THE BEGINNING
RUNNER'S
HANDBOOK

THE PROVEN 13-WEEK
WALK/RUN PROGRAM

IAN MACNEILL AND
THE SPORT MEDICINE COUNCIL
OF BRITISH COLUMBIA

REVISED TEXT BY
SportMedBC's Marnie Caron

GREYSTONE BOOKS

Douglas & McIntyre Publishing Group
Vancouver/Toronto/Berkeley

Greystone Books
A division of Douglas & McIntyre Ltd.
2323 Quebec Street, Suite 201
Vancouver, British Columbia
V5T 4S7
www.greystonebooks.com

Library and Archives Canada Cataloguing in Publication
MacNeill, Ian, 1954-
The beginning runner's handbook : the proven 13-week walk/run
program / Ian MacNeill and the Sport Medicine Council of British Columbia;
revised text by SportMedBC's Marnie Caron. —3rd rev. ed.
Includes bibliographical references and index.

ISBN 1-55365-087-5

1. Running. I. Caron, Marnie II. Sport Medicine Council of B.C.
III. Title. IV. Title: Runner's handbook.
GV502.M32 2005   613.7'17   C2004-906624-2

Library of Congress Cataloguing information is available upon request

Editing of revised text by Anne Rose
Editing of original text by Daphne Gray-Grant
Cover design by Jessica Sullivan
Cover photography by Cathrine Wessel/CORBIS/MAGMA
Interior design by Warren Clark
Illustrations by Warren Clark
Packaged for Greystone Books by House of Words
Printed and bound in Canada by Friesens
Printed on acid-free paper that is forest friendly (100% post-consumer
recycled paper) and has been processed chlorine free
Distributed in the U.S. by Publishers Group West

We gratefully acknowledge the financial support of the
Canada Council for the Arts, the British Columbia Arts Council,
and the government of Canada through the Book Publishing Industry
Development Program (BPIDP) for our publishing activities.

I would like to acknowledge and give thanks
to all of the people who have provided direction, support
and inspiration, with special thanks to
Lynda Cannell, Patricia Chuey, Dr. Doug Clement, Wendy Epp,
Jeanne Gordon, Jackie Halloway, Lynn Kanuka,
Thom Lutes, Jim Miller, Phil Moore,
Denise Morbey, Dr. Karen Nordahl, Cindy O'Krane,
Dallas Parsons, Dr. Trent Smith,
Dr. Jack Taunton, Jerry Tighe and Rachel Turner-Bourne.

MARNIE CARON

Contents

Foreword

IT IS IMPOSSIBLE TO DRIVE DOWN ANY ROAD OR WALK IN A park without being reminded that many people choose running as a way to maintain or improve their health. Running has gained popularity not only because it requires scant equipment and is portable to any site, but because it has been proven to reduce the risk of such conditions as heart disease, high blood pressure, diabetes, obesity and depression. And to get these benefits requires an outlay of just a few hours each week. Small wonder that hundreds of thousands of enthusiasts around the world find running an ideal form of exercise and a good path to physical fitness.

This book is aimed at the would-be runner who needs information about how to become fit. Running appears to be so simple that many individuals approach it thinking success will come easily; beginning runners often get hurt because they train too intensely and too frequently. The moderate, 13-week walk/run program and the guidance offered in this book equip an aspiring runner with the knowledge essential to achieving his or her goal in manageable stages, with minimal risk of injury.

As a former Olympic runner, and coach to dozens of Olympic runners over the past 55 years, I believe in the intrinsic value of running. But as a sport medicine specialist, I know that most of the more than half-million patients entering the clinic with which I am associated have been runners. Had they followed a program like the one presented here, it is far less likely that they would have had to seek medical treatment. This book offers the most concise presentation of information for the beginning runner I have ever seen. I recommend it to every reader as the path to a healthy fitness routine and a more enjoyable life.

Doug Clement, M.D.

Introduction

THIS BOOK WAS WRITTEN SPECIFICALLY FOR *BEGINNING* runners. It has been designed to answer the practical questions you may have about getting started. It will tell you how to avoid sore muscles and injury. It will give you advice about motivation and help you set realistic and achievable goals. And, most important, it will provide you with a recipe for success, a tried and true training program for starting to run.

The heart and soul of this book is the Sport Medicine Council of British Columbia's (SportMedBC) InTraining program, the 13-week walk/run program that has its roots in what is now one of the world's most popular 10-k runs, the *Vancouver Sun* Run™. A relatively obscure event when it started in 1983, the *Sun* Run™ now attracts thousands of runners—nearly 50,000 participated in 2004. But as the run started to grow, event organizers noticed that the frequency of running-related injuries had risen. A good number of the runners were first-timers and many of them hadn't properly trained or prepared for the event. It wasn't until after they were injured that they learned the necessary steps required to safely go the distance. Either that, or they quit altogether.

It seemed clear that many participants would benefit from receiving expert advice *before* the run.

The program presented in this book was originally developed by Dr. Doug Clement, a sport medicine physician, former Canadian national team running coach and recently retired co-director of the Allan McGavin Sport Medicine Centre at the University of British Columbia. After several years of treating a steady stream of running casualties, he decided to design a training plan that neophyte runners could follow and benefit from. The mandate was simple: develop a graduated program that intersperses walking with jogging or running in order to help people develop the physical robustness to run, walk or jog a 10-k course without getting injured.

In 1996, the 13-week program became the basis for a series of community-based running clinics created and administered by SportMedBC. They were made available at local recreation centers, fitness clubs and YMCAs/YWCAs. Although the fundamentals of the program stayed the same (walking interspersed with jogging or running), each training segment was carefully fine-tuned. Over five years, the original training program was then modified to fit the real-life experiences of the more than 35,000 individuals who used the program. Compelled by the testimonials of clinic participants—some of whom claimed that following the program provided one of the most rewarding, life-altering experiences they had ever had—we decided to take the program to a larger audience. Since then, tens of thousands of people worldwide have accomplished their running goals using the *Beginning Runner's Handbook*.

This program has been proven to work by people who may have been fearful at first, but who doggedly set goals and persevered to achieve them. The book includes first-hand accounts from many of these runners—telling about their challenges, setbacks, successes and failures. As well, it includes guidance from a wide range of professionals, all experts in their respective fields of nutrition, sport medicine, sport science, psychology and coaching.

Whether you want to start running to lose weight, relieve stress, quit smoking, reduce your cholesterol levels, meet new people or simply get fitter, this book will help you meet your goal. You will learn how to start an exercise regime the right way, and you will be able to learn from the mistakes and successes of others. Best of all, once you have started the program, you will be able to come back to the book and review specific sections for encouragement, advice and reinforcement. Having the book is a bit like having a personal running coach in your back pocket. If you use a logbook, and we highly recommend that you do, this book will also help serve as a permanent record of your achievement. (See page 192 for a sample logbook page. *The Beginning Runner's Journal,* the companion text to this book, provides a complete logbook. See page 207 for source info.)

A word of caution. As you thumb through the book and flip to the training program itself, you may at first glance think the 13-week walk/run program looks too easy. You may wonder what walking has to do with training to become a runner. The answer is that your bones, ligaments, tendons and muscles require a very slow and gradual buildup to activity, particularly if they haven't seen much action for a while; walking helps prepare them for the stress of running. Although you may be tempted to go out and just start running on your own, or to jump ahead, you should stick to the program. There is no magic potion you can swallow to become a runner, no short cuts to or untold secrets of success. The 13-week program requires dedication and a certain amount of perseverance.

We do know, however, that it works. Even if you have no intention of toeing up to the start line of a race, consider making a commitment to follow the program. At the end of the 13 weeks, not only will you will feel better but you'll be healthier as well. Who knows? You might even become a runner for life.

The following three symbols are used throughout this book:

 Interesting facts about running, fitness and health

 Brief summaries of key information from the text

 Running tips from track-and-field Olympian Lynn Kanuka

Why Run?

ONLY A FEW DECADES AGO, RUNNING WAS CONSIDERED THE sport of oddballs and kooks; few recognized its health benefits. Although today it is widely accepted that fit people are healthier and live longer, it took some rigorous research to prove the point.

One of the first persons to shed light on the exercise/health debate was British researcher J. N. Morris. In the 1960s, he studied the illness rates of conductors and drivers working the London buses, and of mail carriers and their desk-bound counterparts inside post offices. He discovered that the conductors and mail carriers, who were constantly moving, suffered fewer heart attacks than did the more sedentary drivers and clerks. Furthermore, when the conductors and carriers did have heart attacks, they usually survived, whereas the drivers and clerks more often died.

American researcher Ralph Paffenbarger conducted a similar study in 1968, comparing the health of longshoremen with that of dockside office workers. His findings mirrored those of Morris's: the fitter the workers were, the longer they lived. That still left an important question, of course: Why? To appreciate the answer, you need to understand a little bit about how the human body operates.

The Importance of Oxygen

Every living cell in the body requires a constant supply of oxygen. Oxygen is absorbed into the blood via the lungs, then transported throughout the body by means of a system of blood vessels, the largest of which are the veins and arteries, the smallest the capillaries. In addition to inherited health factors, both fitness and diet affect how efficiently a person's oxygen delivery system functions.

Unfortunately, not only are people in the Western world sedentary, they also often have diets high in fat. That fat gets into the bloodstream and lodges in cracks in the arterial walls in a form called plaque. Over time the plaque builds, so that eventually it can block the flow of oxygenated blood to major organs such as the heart and brain as well as to the muscles. If the heart receives too little oxygen, the result can be angina. With angina, which can be very painful, the heart seizes momentarily, but

RUNNER PROFILE

Jack

Jack took up running more than 35 years ago. At the time, he had his heart set on a career as a professional football player and running seemed like a great way to improve his endurance. It wasn't a commonly shared sentiment. "We were definitely the lonely long-distance runners," he recalls. "People used to throw cola bottles at us and try to run us off the road." He participated in the first Vancouver Marathon, in 1972, one of only 32 souls brave enough, or perhaps, some would have said at the time, foolish enough, to do so. Eventually his gridiron dreams receded but his love of running remained.

A sport medicine physician and co-director of a large university sport medicine center, Jack's not sure how he'd get through a week without running. He estimates that so far—he's 59 years old and plans to run at least into his 70s—he's run more than 90,000 miles (144,000 kilometers) and participated in more than 60 marathons, and he's still going strong.

recovers its momentum when the supply of oxygen kicks in again. But if the flow of oxygen is cut off for long enough, the result will be a myocardial infarction, or as it's more commonly known, a heart attack.

Another consequence of poor circulation can be a blockage of blood to the brain, leading to a stroke. With a mild stroke, parts of an oxygen-deprived brain simply die off, often resulting in paralysis or the loss of certain functions. A more extensive stroke can be fatal.

Our muscles also need oxygen for almost everything they do. Generally, the harder the work, the more oxygen they need. But sudden surges of energy, such as that needed by someone fleeing from a grizzly bear, for example, require hardly any oxygen at all. That's because the body has more than one way of producing energy.

The aerobic and anaerobic systems

The word "aerobic" means "in the presence of oxygen." You are operating aerobically when you walk, sit, sleep, eat, watch television or read a book, and, ideally, when you exercise ("ideally" because when your body operates aerobically, it can produce energy to keep you going for a long time). In the simplest terms, you produce energy aerobically when the air you breathe works together with the food you eat to make your muscles operate. It's similar to the way gas and air work together to make a car's engine go.

Sometimes your body is called upon to do strenuous work very quickly—for example, to help you flee when you suddenly find yourself between a bear and her cubs. To have any chance of escaping, you will have to come up

 The normal adult human heart beats about 40 million times a year. Each day, your heart circulates 4,000 U.S. gallons (15,000 liters) of blood through your body. Your heart is a muscle. To strengthen it, you must exercise it, just as you would any other muscle in your body.

with a lot of energy almost instantly. That's when your anaerobic system is likely to kick in. As the name suggests, anaerobic means "in the absence of oxygen." Unlike the aerobic system, which requires oxygen to produce energy, the anaerobic system uses the fuel stored in the muscles.

Day to day, your body gets its energy from a mix of aerobic and anaerobic sources. The more intense the activity and the more your body's demand for oxygen exceeds your ability to supply it, the more you work anaerobically. That's why when you're engaged in intense activity, your breathing accelerates: your body is trying to get more of that precious oxygen and remain aerobic.

Everyone, even a highly trained athlete, works anaerobically in certain situations. A wide receiver going for a

RUNNER PROFILE

Wendy

At 35, Wendy was a flight attendant and the mother of two toddlers. She had been a runner most of her adult life when the difficult birth of her second child caused severe sciatic nerve damage, resulting in drop-foot—paralysis from the knee down. She had to wear a brace just to walk, and in time her good knee began to buckle as it tried to compensate for the other's weakness. Not a quitter, Wendy signed up for a 13-week walk/run clinic. At first, the pain was excruciating, but having followed a weight-training program designed by her run leader, she was soon running three times a week for up to an hour each time. Her ultimate goal was to compete in a marathon.

"It was really helpful with the babies, both for running away from them and for catching them," she says with a laugh. "It was important for my mental health as well. You can get bogged down in things, then you can go for a run and come back feeling completely refreshed. There's such a sense of accomplishment; you're on your own and all you need is a pair of shoes."

pass in a football game, for example, will produce energy anaerobically when he is sprinting down the sideline in pursuit of the ball. As you become fitter, however, you will push up your "anaerobic threshold," the point at which your body switches over to anaerobic-based energy sources.

The reason you want to push up your anaerobic threshold is that if you are getting your energy from mainly anaerobic sources, you can't keep up any activity for very long. Depending on how fit you are, your anaerobic energy supply will last from 5 to 60 seconds. Obviously that's not enough to allow you to run around the block, let alone run 10 k.

Another reason to prolong the amount of time you work aerobically is that the chemical reactions taking place in your body during anaerobic exercise produce accumulations of lactic acid in the working muscles. Researchers think this byproduct is the cause of the soreness in muscles following bouts of strenuous exercise. Again, depending on how fit you are, your body will take a day or more to break down and eliminate the lactic acid.

Feeling a little stiff and sore after a workout isn't entirely bad; it's part of the process that will make you fitter. Still, the 13-week walk/run program will slowly increase your tolerance for exercise while keeping your body working aerobically as much as possible. As you gradually train yourself, you will find you are able to function more efficiently (that is, aerobically) at higher workloads.

 Running not only strengthens your heart but also "trains" your endothelium, which is the lining of your blood vessels. A more flexible endothelium, brought about by exercise, means your heart won't have to work as hard to pump blood to your muscles.

Running is good for your skin. Running stimulates circulation, transporting nutrients and flushing out waste products. The result is less subcutaneous fat and clearer skin.

Exercise and Health

How does being fit make you healthier?

The blood vessels of a fit person tend to accumulate less plaque than those of an unfit person, leading to a lower risk of heart attack or stroke. Additionally, a person who exercises will improve his or her circulatory system in general, in part by making the lining of the blood vessels more flexible, so that the heart doesn't have to work as hard to pump the blood through the body. The result is that even if there are blockages in the blood vessels, the circulation around those blockages will improve. (There's still some debate about whether you can actually reduce the amount of plaque that's already built up in your system, but the question might be moot if you can improve the circulation around it.)

Over time, as you exercise regularly you increase the number of capillaries in your muscles (the small blood vessels that deliver nutrients and remove wastes), as well as the number of mitochondria (living particles inside cells that produce energy) and the enzymes in those mitochondria that allow you to function aerobically.

Exercise stimulates the body to produce endorphins, the body's natural painkillers. Endorphins are remarkably similar in structure to morphine, and there's some evidence that people get addicted to running because they are hooked on the endorphin rush. There are less healthy things to be hooked on!

Moderate exercise also seems to boost the immune system, apparently by improving the killer T-cell function. These cells are the army ants of your immune system; they rush in and kill invaders. (But note that if you exercise until your body is thoroughly fatigued, you can actually impair killer T-cell function. During the 24 to 48 hours following exhaustive exercise—a marathon, for example—you are more susceptible to upper respiratory system infections, such as colds.)

Finally, exercise reduces stress. It does this by allowing the body to metabolize the stress hormone adrenaline more quickly. Adrenaline is one of nature's mixed blessings, vital to get you through crises but debilitating if there's too much of it or if it sticks around too long. Better regulation of the amount of adrenaline in your system is another potential health benefit of exercise.

 Running lowers your blood pressure and your resting heart rate while raising your "good" cholesterol levels.

More Reasons to Get Fit

Regular exercise provides a great incentive for adopting a healthier lifestyle—eating a low-fat diet, getting proper rest, forgoing cigarettes—because doing so makes exercise easier and more pleasant.

Exercise can help you control your weight. Many people seem to put on weight as they age. Some argue it's because the metabolism slows with age; others say the only reason the metabolism slows down is that people become less active as they get older. (Then again, some people remain slim their entire lives and never seem to do a stick of work.) What is known for certain is that most people find that a regular exercise program—combined with healthy eating habits—can help ward off extra pounds. And speaking of exercise and food, there's a little bonus built into life for people who exercise. Even if weight is not an issue for you, doing more exercise (that is, burning more calories) opens up room in your diet for more of the things you love to eat that would otherwise add inches to your waistline, hips or buttocks.

Fit people have a better self-image, partly because they look and feel better and partly because they have more confidence in their ability to be active. Perhaps this is the basis for the belief that fit people make better lovers!

In any case, getting fit will make you stronger, so you can enjoy participating in a broader range of physical activities. If you're the kind of person who cringes in fear when one of the kids suggests going to the park and kicking a ball around, getting in shape can improve not only your life but your children's as well. Active parents encourage a more active lifestyle in their children, not just when the kids are young but in all the years to come.

RUNNER PROFILE

Colin

After returning home from a holiday in Scotland, Colin was feeling despondent. Giving in to Scottish hospitality had caused his weight to go way up. The then 42-year-old airport ground handler didn't like the idea of perpetually hauling around 265 pounds (120 kilos). "I mentioned it to a friend and he said it was no problem. He was training for a marathon, so why didn't I just train for the half marathon?"

At first Colin balked. "I told him, 'Forget it, running is not for me.' But the seed was planted." He trained for five months, lost close to 45 pounds (20 kilos) and felt as if his life had been transformed. "Running changed my life, and not just from the perspective of being able to run." What resonates for Colin is how training has altered his view of his own abilities. "It's what happens when you're out on the road and you're pushing it in the middle of a race and you have to dig down really deep to make sure you cross the finish line," he says. "That really epitomizes life to me. Running isn't just a sport, it's a philosophy you can apply to all parts of your life."

The Joy of Running

Aerobic exercise increases the heart rate and thereby helps to improve your cardiovascular system, stave off heart disease and improve circulation and muscle tone. It can provide you with more energy, perhaps help you lose weight, probably make you sleep better and certainly make you look and feel a lot better about yourself. But of all the possible forms of aerobic activity, why choose running?

For starters, running is one of the least expensive sports. Once you invest in a good pair of shoes, you're done. Compare this with the cost of golf, skiing, hockey or even tennis. With running, there are no pads to wear, green fees to pay, lift tickets to buy or balls to wear out.

Running is also easy to get involved in. All it takes is a pair of good shoes, a little time and a healthy dose of motivation. You can do it practically anywhere. Some people like to run alongside busy streets, others on tree-shaded park trails. Some like to jog along the beach at sunset; some run in the dead of night between deserted skyscrapers. You can run alone just as easily as in the middle of a pack. You can go the competitive route and enter races, or spend the rest of your life in pursuit of personal goals, never bothering to check your time and distance, simply running for the sheer joy and benefits of it.

You can run your whole life. With proper conditioning, your body will run a long time, well into old age.

Running is something you can do with friends or alone. You don't need other people the way you do with tennis, racquetball, soccer, hockey, basketball or Frisbee.

Excessive pooling of blood in the legs because of inactivity may cause varicose veins. Exercise can help by providing for the efficient return of venous blood to the heart after it has been pumped to other parts of your body.

You don't have to wait for someone to meet you, then feel stuck when the person doesn't show up. You can warm up, run for 20 minutes, cool down, shower and get on with the rest of your day, just like that.

If you do choose to run by yourself, running can give you something you may have difficulty finding in your life: time to get away from it all and be alone with your own thoughts. If you have a busy career and/or a growing family, you can sometimes feel pretty squeezed. Everybody needs some time alone and running can give you that time.

Alternatively, running can help you make new friends. If you choose to join a running group, you will meet people you might never have met in other circumstances—people whose other interests in life are entirely

RUNNER PROFILE

Paul

When Paul was approaching 50, his life took a downturn. "I had severe allergies, I developed rheumatoid arthritis and all of a sudden I had a nervous breakdown," the now 56-year-old salesman says.

Deeply concerned for his health and well-being, both his doctor and his psychiatrist recommended more exercise. Paul joined a walking club, which not only got him moving but helped break down the emotional barriers he'd built up around himself. Finding himself at the front of the walking pack eventually gave him the confidence to start running, and soon afterward the dividends of exercise and a healthier lifestyle started rolling in. "Running helped me get a grip on my arthritis and gave me the energy to recover from my depression. It also helped me stop distancing myself from other people."

Today, Paul thinks of running as the thread that helps tie his life together. "The bad things that happened to me were kind of a wake-up call. I'd still like to lose some weight and run a little faster," he says with a chuckle, "but at least I haven't put on any more weight and I'm running faster now than if I'd never started."

different from yours. Doctors run with dockworkers who run with flight attendants who run with writers who run with factory workers, and so on. People who run together accept each other as equals.

Running can teach you a lot about who you are. It can show you your limitations and give you the opportunity to move past them. If you keep raising the bar, running can give you the tremendous feeling that bars were made to be raised. Running takes commitment, determination, desire, hard work and a sense of self-worth. Think how many other areas in your life could benefit from your having these attributes.

 People who are physically fit usually have lower heart rates and blood pressure levels. They are less susceptible to the effects of stress, which causes heart rate and blood pressure to rise.

Getting Ready to Run

MOST PEOPLE CAN LACE UP THEIR SHOES AND START A running program without worrying about bringing on a heart attack, aggravating a bad back or provoking some other medical catastrophe. A small percentage, however, should consult a doctor before starting on any fitness regimen, whether or not it includes running.

One way to decide if you need medical supervision is to take a physical readiness test. The Canadian Society for Exercise Physiology has developed a good one, called the Physical Activity Readiness Questionnaire, or PAR-Q, for short (see page 30). If you get through the questionnaire without answering yes to any of the questions—and it's in your best interest to answer them honestly—then you can probably start an exercise program without fear of hurting yourself.

If, however, you answer yes to one or more of these questions, you should talk to your doctor before proceeding.

If you want to get a more accurate assessment of your physical condition, ask your doctor to do a Physical Activity Readiness Medical Examination (the PARmed-X, for short) with you. This special checklist includes useful advice on what types of exercises can safely be done by persons with certain underlying physical conditions. There's even a special screening tool for pregnant women considering an exercise program. Pregnancy rarely makes exercise inadvisable, but it's wise to check with a qualified professional.

The Three Rules of Exercise

Once you're cleared to start an exercise program, it's time to memorize the three rules of exercise: moderation, consistency and rest. They're simple rules, and if you live by them you will find that moving from a sedentary life to an active one can be quite enjoyable rather than a trip through training hell. You will also go a long way toward avoiding injuries, which can undo months, even years, of work.

Marcel

Marcel had his first heart attack when he was just 57. "I guess if you want to look on the bright side," he says, "it was something of a wake-up call." An avid tennis player, Marcel figured he'd be taking it pretty easy for the rest of his life after he collapsed in the shower following a particularly tough tennis match. "I always knew exercise was the way to prevent heart disease, but I figured once you went down you had to sort of back off."

His doctor disagreed and told him the prescription for a long life lay in changing his lifestyle and stopping his habit of exercising in fits and starts. "He told me I could do a lot more exercise than I was used to; it was just a matter of building up to it slowly and doing a few other things differently in my life." Those other things included spending less time in restaurants and more time at the gym. He was referred to a nutritionist, who overhauled his diet, and six months after his heart attack he was much healthier, running three times a week and playing a stronger tennis game than ever.

"You know, I used to spend a lot of time going to restaurants and drinking, and at first I missed all that. Now, on Fridays, instead of going to the bar I tell people I have to get up early to go running."

Of course, living by the three rules will not make you invulnerable to pain or injury. But these rules will help ease you to a higher level of fitness by subjecting your body to the proper amount of stress.

Rule 1: Be moderate

Start slowly. Even if you already have a good level of cardiovascular fitness from other sports, you should follow this advice. Being able to cycle in the Tour de France or swim the English Channel doesn't make you a runner. Even experienced runners (and walkers) need to take care not to overstress themselves. That's because there are special musculoskeletal stresses peculiar to running.

The cardiovascular system is considerably more robust than the musculoskeletal system. Given a reasonable amount of stress, it will respond eagerly, quickly strengthening and giving you the ability to transport more oxygen to hungry muscles. Unfortunately, your bones, ligaments, tendons and muscles are not quite as adaptable. According to Dr. Tim Noakes, a medical research director at the University of Cape Town and author of *Lore of Running,* "If you're reasonably athletic, after six months or so of training you could technically run in a marathon, but your bones wouldn't bc up to it yet." He says the majority of people who haven't been very active are susceptible to bone-stress fractures in the first three to six months if they continually push their training. In other words, while your heart and lungs may be urging you to go, your bones, ligaments, tendons and muscles may want you to ease up.

A large number of well-intentioned people derail their fitness programs by being immoderate. Many of them make a New Year's resolution to get in shape and

Three basic rules of training

1. **Moderation**
   Train gradually, to give your body time to adapt to the stress
2. **Consistency**
   Try not to skip a training day
3. **Rest**
   Ensure at least one rest day between training days

One benefit of running and fitness is a well-tuned immune system that will do a better job of helping your body fight off invading bacteria, viruses and toxins.

crowd the fitness centers during the first couple of weeks of January, but drop out by the time spring rolls around. Those who aren't injured grow discouraged by the punishing pace to which they've subjected themselves.

Although the human body can withstand a great deal of stress, to avoid injury this stress needs to be applied gradually. That's why we advise you to not jump ahead in the training program described in this book, even if it seems somewhat "lightweight" to you in the beginning. Skipping ahead will not make you fit faster, but it will significantly increase the risk that you will be sidelined with sore muscles and joints, or worse.

Rule 2: Be consistent

If moderation is the first rule of training, consistency is the second. Those who break Rule 1 invariably break Rule 2. Here's the pattern. You decide to get in shape, so you head for the gym or go for as long a run as you can endure, and for the next week you feel as though you've been run over by a truck. By the time you've recovered enough to take another stab at it, you push yourself to the wall again to make up for lost time. This kind of training isn't training at all. It's doing you more harm than good, and because it makes you feel worse rather than better, it isn't long before common sense kicks in and undermines your commitment. Eventually you quit.

The virtues of consistency cannot be overstated. When you work out consistently, your body has more time to adapt to the stress of training. What's more, if you are consistent, you won't have to make up for lost time. A day or two of extra-hard work will not make up for those missed training sessions. Instead, you are more likely to overstress your body and find yourself back at square one—or, worse, facing an illness or injury.

As well, the longer you spend developing a solid fitness base, the more secure it is, which means you can take a break every now and then without blowing your whole game plan.

If you think carefully about Rules 1 and 2, it's easy to see why fit people make training part of their lives. The idea that training never ends may seem daunting in the beginning, especially if you find your first efforts difficult. But once your body and mind begin to benefit from exercise, you will find yourself craving it. Instead of forcing yourself to do it, you'll be worrying about when you are going to get the chance. Fit people typically reach stages in their day or week when they are champing at the bit to tie on their shoes and go.

Rule 3: Give your body time to rest

Rest gives your body time and energy to adapt to the changes you bring to it by training. Once your body has adapted, you'll be stronger and more efficient. Build time for rest and recovery into your training plan and be sure to space your workouts over the entire week, not pile them up in a few days.

Think of rest the same way you think of your training sessions—as a conscious physical activity essential to your program and your well-being. Rest is not the avoidance of work; it is a proper period of recovery from an activity that wears your body down.

What about my technique?

- Walking and jogging are the most natural things we do, but our technique is uniquely individual

- The best running technique for you will evolve as you get stronger and possibly incorporate a few running exercises to develop strength

- It is important to use your arms when walking or jogging; your arms dictate your pace

- If you consciously think about your arm action, your leg action will follow

—*Olympian Lynn Kanuka*

Where to Run

One of the great things about running is that you can do it practically anywhere—on a road, in a park, around a track, across the country or on the spot. Nonetheless, if you have a choice, running on softer surfaces will reduce the stress and strain on bones, ligaments, tendons and muscles and make your run more enjoyable all around.

As a running surface, asphalt is preferable to concrete and dirt is better yet because it will absorb more of the impact. If concrete, which does not absorb any impact, is the worst surface, grass or rubberized tracks are probably the best, mainly because they absorb the most. Some runners find tracks boring. On the other hand, grass can hide holes or tree roots that can make you trip. Consider your options carefully.

RUNNER PROFILE

Anna

Anna knows all about what happens if you go too fast too soon and your body isn't prepared for the effort, especially when you have a pre-existing condition that can aggravate the situation. Although she'd always had lower back problems, the then 35-year-old recreation therapist didn't think they would affect her efforts to complete the 13-week walk/run program. As it turns out, she was painfully wrong. About halfway into the program one of her knees became unable to compensate for the alignment problems that started in her back. "I was totally devastated," she recalls. "I thought running just wasn't my sport."

She was going to quit the program altogether, but instead changed to the walking program (see Appendix B) for a few weeks and visited a physiotherapist, who got her swimming and cycling to strengthen the knee. "I went back to the running program in about three weeks. Although I was used to being at the front of the running pack when I first started, I had to get used to the idea of pulling up the rear, but I didn't mind at all. I found myself with all the people who had joined the program for social reasons, thinking, 'Hey, if we finish it, great.' They were all really supportive."

Anna managed to complete the running program with her original group and shortly thereafter went on to complete a 10-k race in 1:20. "I'm so glad it worked out the way it did. I would never have thought I could come back like that."

The Problem with Feet

Footwear has come a long way in the last 20 years, and today's modern shoes can not only help counter various foot flaws but also absorb a lot of the shock to which running subjects your body. Even though barefoot running has briefly caught on as a fad from time to time, most people need good footwear.

Phil Moore, a shoe retailer with so much expertise that he co-authored a scientific paper on athletic footwear, believes that the human foot is remarkably well adapted to the work required of it. "In terms of mechanics, the rear foot and forefoot are working on different planes. As you land on your heel and go into the mid-stance, the foot acts like a loose bag of bones. It does this both to absorb the shock and to adapt to various anomalies in the surface you are running on. When it operates efficiently and properly and there aren't any obtuse angles that shouldn't be there, the foot works really well."

Unfortunately, not all feet work equally well. Moore says that about 95 per cent of the problem feet he sees are afflicted by overpronation, which is a tendency for the foot to roll too far inward. (Notice that the problem is *over*pronation. The foot pronates naturally. If it didn't, it would have a tough time absorbing the shock of running.)

The overpronated foot can cause several problems, both in the foot itself and in the rest of the leg, not to mention in the lower back. Before the design of footwear became the science it is today, overpronated feet were called flat feet, and people with such feet were often kept out of the army because they couldn't walk or run long distances. If you stand up and artificially flatten your feet,

Pronation is the flattening of your foot's arch during weight bearing, causing the foot to roll inward. Some pronation is normal and allows your foot to absorb shock. Excessive pronation, however, will strain your foot, knee, leg, thigh and hip.

Supination occurs when your foot's arch fails to flatten out enough during weight bearing. If you suffer from excess supination—a rare condition—you'll tend to walk on the outside edges of your feet.

you'll notice that your knees start pointing inward. If you run that way, your knees will track poorly and joint problems could develop. A flat foot also compresses the lower back and can lead to back pain.

The opposite of pronation is supination, which occurs when the foot's arch fails to flatten out enough during weight bearing. If you have this rare condition, you'll tend to walk on the outside edges of your feet.

Some people start out with good feet but life plays havoc with them. For example, the weight of pregnancy can cause a woman's feet to flatten, especially if she regularly wears sandals. Often, people don't notice flaws in their feet when they are young and flexible, but when those people get older or put more stress on their feet by running, the flaws become apparent.

Choosing a Good Shoe

When you run, each foot strikes the ground somewhere between 800 and 1,200 times per mile (500 and 750 times per kilometer). In the beginning, you will be coming down on your feet with one and one-half to two times your body weight, but when you get faster the impact can increase to four times your body weight. For that reason alone your footwear needs increased cushioning throughout, particularly in the heel. It also has to provide good support for the foot and arch. Women should remember that they generally have narrower feet than men and might have trouble fitting securely into men's shoes. Fortunately, shoe manufacturers have recognized this market. Every good running shoe company now offers separate styles for men and women. And some, such as New Balance, also offer shoes in various widths.

You may already have had hints of foot problems. Perhaps you never seem to be able to buy shoes that feel right, or you develop various pains in your feet, legs or lower body if you walk for any length of time. Today there is likely a shoe to help you overcome your problems. The best way to find the right shoe for you is to go to a good running store and have your foot measured properly by a running shoe expert. Once you have this information, you will be better able to choose the correct shoe style for your feet.

Stable shoes that correct or support the alignment of your feet will help you to run efficiently and without pain. If your feet overpronate, you need shoes that provide extra support so that your feet don't flatten out too much. Sometimes there's enough support in the shoes; sometimes you have to add some kind of orthotic (shoe insert), which can be prescribed by a sport physician or podiatrist. When you do find shoes that work for you, you'll probably want to stick with that model as long as it is available because people often develop problems just after switching to another type of shoe.

In choosing shoes, it's also important to think about the type of surface you run on. If you have a normal or "neutral" foot, you still might want a shoe with more support if you run on trails or other uneven ground, where there is more chance of twisting an ankle.

Shoe quality varies considerably; no two pairs are identical. (It's said that cars made on Mondays and Fridays have more defects and the same is probably true when it comes to shoes.) Inspect shoes carefully before buying and ask your retailer about the return policy for defective ones, because defects often show up only after the shoe is put to the test of use. If you're not happy with the retailer's policy,

What to look for in a shoe

"Normal" foot
Stability shoe with moderate control features and a semi-curved last (inner sole)

"Flat" foot
Motion control or stability shoe, with a firm midsole and a straight or semi-curved last

High-arched foot
Cushioned shoe with good flexibility (stay away from motion control shoes) and a curved last

shop somewhere else; most manufacturers of better-quality running shoes offer a warranty on their product. After you take your shoes home, remember to inspect them regularly so that you spot deterioration before it can cause a running injury.

Walking puts less stress on your feet than running, but walking in the wrong type of shoes will also lead to misery. Your feet support you and carry you for miles, not only when you're walking for exercise but through every step of your life. Comfortable, flexible, lightweight walking shoes, with a cushioned sole, good arch support, a firm heel counter and a little extra room for your toes, are a very worthwhile investment.

Choosing Your Clothing

Clothing is not the most important consideration when you run, but it's not irrelevant either. What you wear should be primarily a function of weather. Stores offer a lot of flashy running gear, but consider comfort first.

If you're lucky enough to live in a climate that's neither too hot nor too cold, you want to avoid overdressing. Your body will heat up when you run and a jacket that's

RUNNER PROFILE

Brenda

Brenda had been running off and on for 20 years but she could never get herself to last more than half an hour—until the then 48-year-old counselor went through the 13-week walk/run program. "It worked for me because it added on just a little bit more each time," she says.

Getting more proficient at running also helped her get more control over her life and feel better about who she is. "Not only is it a good way to keep the weight down, but you feel so good after it's done. I have a full-time job and two children, and after a day of doing for everyone else, running is something I can do for me and me alone, even if it's only for half an hour."

Although she had never thought of herself as an athlete, Brenda went on to train for a half marathon.

cozy when you start out will feel suffocating when you reach running temperature. When you overheat you tend to lose a lot of body fluid through sweat, thereby dehydrating yourself. It's a good idea to layer clothes so that you can adjust the layers to suit weather conditions. You will quickly discover that a sweat-soaked cotton T-shirt plastered to your body feels as unpleasant as it looks.

In the last 10 years there have been tremendous improvements in running and exercise clothing. Today, technical athletic clothing is primarily made of synthetic fibers, and you can find lightweight running shirts, sports bras, shorts and tights made from multiple layers of nylon- and polyester-based materials. According to Phil Moore, owner of Vancouver's LadySport running store, "The weaves and textures of these fabrics are designed to wick moisture away from the skin, rather than absorbing it into the garment itself. Cotton, on the other hand, can absorb up to seven times its weight in water, resulting in clothing that is colder in winter, warmer in summer and very heavy when wet. Cotton also fades, stretches and shrinks." As well, says Moore, "The new materials use hydrophilic/hydrophobic layers, magnet technology, silver fibers and multiple densities of stitch counts to effect moisture movement, temperature management, breathability and support." All of these improvements make running in any temperature and climate easier and more enjoyable.

Female runners will probably want to consider a sport bra, as physical activity causes the breasts to bounce. The breast is supported by a fragile structure of skin and ligaments that can be stretched by bouncing, leading to breast sag. Most everyday bras will not stop this bouncing. Enter the sports bra. Today's sports bras are well designed and even serve as outerwear, making them a great option in hot

The runner's wardrobe

Socks Synthetic fiber

Shorts Comfortable, synthetic fiber

Shirt Synthetic fiber

Jacket Lightweight, water-resistant, breathable fabric

Cotton may be 100 per cent natural, but it's not a fiber you want next to your body when you're sweating because it holds in moisture. Instead, look for synthetic fabrics that wick moisture away from your body.

weather. Look for a snug fit (to control motion) and a design that minimizes movement within the bra (to eliminate chafing). Large-breasted women should look for molded cups; smaller-breasted women can go with the compression type bras that flatten the breasts. Fabric should be a 50 per cent blend of cotton and some form of breathable material, such as Lycra. Avoid cups with seams that can irritate the nipple, and make sure any hardware is adequately cushioned. You'll want wide straps, because all that motion can make narrow straps slip off the shoulders. Finally, be sure your arms have enough room to move freely.

Many people love running in the cold because it helps keep body temperature down and some days it seems one could run forever. Still, you don't want to get too cold. Outerwear should be a breathable fabric such as Gore-Tex (numerous imitators function equally well), which is also water repellent. Keep in mind that no matter how breathable the fabric, if you work up enough of a sweat you will overwhelm its ability to dissipate the moisture. A raised collar will help protect your neck, which can be especially sensitive in the cold; consider wearing a turtleneck. Synthetic undergarments can add extra warmth. And since as much as 70 per cent of body heat is lost through your head, consider a hat, too. Gloves can keep your hands from feeling like they're freezing solid. If you wear socks (some runners don't), look for a fabric that will wick away moisture. Some runners avoid blistering by wearing two pairs of thin socks that can rub against each other instead of against sensitive skin.

Setting Goals

People successful in any area of life, including sports and careers, share one common characteristic—they set realistic and meaningful goals for themselves. No one can safely compete in a 10 k one week after they begin training.

Your mind, like your body, has to adjust to new levels of effort. If you set unrealistic goals for yourself and fail to achieve them, you will almost certainly become discouraged and perhaps quit. Why not set realistic goals for yourself to begin with and train your mind the same way you train your body? In the 13-week walk/run program, the goals are set out for you and the program is tried and true. Make a commitment to follow it and you are likely to succeed.

This doesn't mean you won't have lapses of confidence or motivation as you progress through the program. Becoming a runner takes the kind of effort against which most of our minds and bodies are inclined to rebel. But the 13-week program is designed to train your mind at the same time as it trains your body, so that you can face and move past the inevitable trials.

Words of advice from those who have "been there"

- **Start slowly.** Follow the training schedule!
- **Go at your own pace.** Don't be pressured to run or walk faster than you are comfortable with.
- **Think positively.** Focus on what feels good, not on what hurts.
- **Make time to work out.** Set aside a specific time for your workouts and protect this time so that other commitments don't interfere with your training.
- **Congratulate yourself.** After a workout, stop and think about how good you feel. Remember this feeling the next time you're not too keen about heading out.

Physical Activity Readiness
Questionnaire - PAR-Q
(revised 1994)

PAR - Q & YOU

(A Questionnaire for People Aged 15 to 69)

Regular physical activity is fun and healthy, and increasingly more people are starting to become more active every day. Being mo active is very safe for most people. However, some people should check with their doctor before they start becoming much mo physically active.

If you are planning to become much more physically active than you are now, start by answering the seven questions in the box below. you are between the ages of 15 and 69, the PAR-Q will tell you if you should check with your doctor before you start. If you are over 69 yea of age, and you are not used to being very active, check with your doctor.

Common sense is your best guide when you answer these questions. Please read the questions carefully and answer each one honestl check YES or NO.

YES	NO		
☐	☐	1.	Has your doctor ever said that you have a heart condition <u>and</u> that you should only do physical activity recommended by a doctor?
☐	☐	2.	Do you feel pain in your chest when you do physical activity?
☐	☐	3.	In the past month, have you had chest pain when you were not doing physical activity?
☐	☐	4.	Do you lose your balance because of dizziness or do you ever lose consciousness?
☐	☐	5.	Do you have a bone or joint problem that could be made worse by a change in your physical activity?
☐	☐	6.	Is your doctor currently prescribing drugs (for example, water pills) for your blood pressure or heart condition?
☐	☐	7.	Do you know of <u>any other reason</u> why you should not do physical activity?

If
you
answered

YES to one or more questions

Talk with your doctor by phone or in person BEFORE you start becoming much more physically active or BEFORE you have a fitness appraisal. Tell your doctor about the PAR-Q and which questions you answered YES.

- You may be able to do any activity you want — as long as you start slowly and build up gradually. Or, you may need to restric your activities to those which are safe for you. Talk with your doctor about the kinds of activities you wish to participate in and follow his/her advice.
- Find out which community programs are safe and helpful for you.

NO to all questions

If you answered NO honestly to <u>all</u> PAR-Q questions, you can be reasonably sure that you can:

- start becoming much more physically active — begin slowly and build up gradually. This is the safest and easiest way to go.
- take part in a fitness appraisal — this is an excellent way to determine your basic fitness so that you can plan the best way for you to live actively.

DELAY BECOMING MUCH MORE ACTIVE:

- if you are not feeling well because of a temporary illness suc as a cold or a fever — wait until you feel better; or
- if you are or may be pregnant — talk to your doctor before yo start becoming more active.

Please note: If your health changes so that you then answer YES t any of the above questions, tell your fitness or health professional Ask whether you should change your physical activity plan.

<u>Informed Use of the PAR-Q</u>: The Canadian Society for Exercise Physiology, Health Canada, and their agents assume no liability for persons who undertake physical activity, a if in doubt after completing this questionnaire, consult your doctor prior to physical activity.

Printed by permission of the Canadian Society for Exercise Physiology

3

On the Road

THE 13-WEEK WALK/RUN PROGRAM IS A TEMPLATE FOR fitness that has been used successfully by thousands of people to prepare for one of the largest running/walking events in North America, the *Vancouver Sun* Run™. The training schedule you will follow (see page 151) starts off slowly to help you build strength, stamina and confidence. Your focus over the next 13 weeks will be to improve your overall health and fitness while remaining injury free. If possible, find a friend or a group of friends to train with you; it's not only more fun with friends, it's more motivating.

Each training session is broken down into five-minute components. These blocks are long enough to lead to improvement, but not so onerous that you will feel exhausted or sore. There's a psychological benefit as well: the tasks in each block are relatively easy to complete, which will give you the confidence to go on.

Study the program carefully to see where you will be going and how long it will take you to get there. It's important to remember that the times noted for the training sessions do not include the time you will have to spend warming up and cooling down. For most of the program, the five-minute blocks are divided into walking and

✔ Pace your training session on windy days by running *into* the wind when you start and still have lots of energy. Come home with the wind at your back.

running; as the weeks pass, the ratio of running to walking increases, until by the last week you are just running. As early as the second or third week you may start to feel quite comfortable with the workouts and may feel ready to jump ahead. But your bones, ligaments, tendons and muscles adapt to training much less quickly than your cardiovascular system; to stay injury free, you must give them time to catch up. Getting injured halfway through the program would be far more discouraging than taking the prescribed time to get to the continuous running stage.

Schedule enough time each week to complete the three training sessions with rest days in between, rather than trying to squeeze your training sessions into consecutive days. Many people find it helps to start on a weekend. It also helps to pick a running route that's enticing, and as free of obstacles—pedestrians and cars—as possible. Think of running an "out-and-back route," and at the halfway point, head back home.

One piece of equipment you will definitely need is a sport watch with a stopwatch feature. Digital is best; sweep second-hand readings tend to get approximated when you're bouncing along.

Keeping a Training Log

Many fitness enthusiasts keep training logs, and athletes often have daily training records going back 10 years or more. These records allow them to see the big picture, the patterns that emerge only over time. If you decide to keep a training log, you may find it a hassle at first, but if you keep detailed notes on such things as diet and sleep patterns, how much time you spent warming up and stretching, and when, where and how far you ran, it will allow you to see a new, healthier pattern starting to form in your life.

You may find you even start recording your thoughts, a practice that can really pay dividends. Many runners say their moments of greatest clarity come when they are running, and you may find your insights worth recalling at a later date. At the very least, a year or two down the road you can look back at your old training logs and laugh when you see an entry describing how you maxed out at 545 yards (500 meters) of running—when today you can knock off 5 k without breaking a sweat. (Refer to Appendix A— page 192—for an example of how you can use a logbook to record your training progress.)

Many people find that keeping a journal is motivating. If you're having a tough time getting up off the couch, try picking up your training log and flipping through the pages summarizing all your hard work. Then look at the next, blank page—the one that can't be filled in until after that day's training session. Most of the time this will be enough to get you lacing up your shoes.

Keeping a training log in which you record aches and pains can also help you to prevent injuries, or, if not, at least to better recover from them. Noting your aches and pains may motivate you to deal with their causes before they lead to actual injuries. And if you *do* become injured, the log will allow you to work more closely with your doctor or physiotherapist, detailing the kinds of problems you've been having and how they originally manifested themselves.

In a nutshell, keeping a training log will enable you to:

- analyze the effects of your training
- monitor your progress

 Muscles can be stretched further when warm, which is why you should do your "deep" stretching exercises *after* rather than before your run.

Consider jotting down notes about your diet in your training log. Having a record of food intake can help you identify problem times, moods or stresses that affect your eating. And you'll be able to see how all of these things affect your training.

- develop a systematic plan for improvement
- avoid overtraining and injury
- stay motivated
- look back in wonder, amusement or perhaps even amazement

Warming Up

No matter how motivated you are, if running or brisk walking has not been part of your daily life, your body will find exercise something of a shock. The 13-week walk/run program is designed to minimize the shock, but the need for warm-up exercises before every training session cannot be overemphasized. Warming up is *not* just for beginners—even world-class athletes need to warm up before every workout.

Malcolm

Malcolm, 43, has been keeping a training log for 25 years. "It started when I first started running, because every book on running I ever read said you should keep one," says the marketing and communications director. "Eventually I just got hooked on it." Because Malcolm runs every day—not something you should consider at this stage of your running career—he writes in his journal every day. This means that after 25-odd years of running and writing, he has a box full of notebooks. He found the log especially useful when he first started running because all those blank pages staring him in the face made him feel accountable.

He writes everything in his log, he says: where he ran and for how long, how he felt, what the weather was like, what he ate that day. "It's all there: whether I felt okay or good or really good or ridiculously good, or ridiculously bad, for that matter. It's great, because you know how it is in normal life—somebody asks you what you did two months ago and you can hardly remember, whereas if you've kept a diary you can look back and see exactly what you did two months ago. It gives you a clear definition of where you are versus where you've been."

The purpose of a warm-up routine is to prepare your body for exercise. (Warming up itself should not be thought of as exercise, even if the routines are called warm-up "exercises.") Cold muscles work less efficiently and are more easily injured. They lack the flow of blood necessary to do the work called for by exercise.

Your warm-up should include some kind of general body movement designed to get the blood flowing. After about 10 minutes of moving your arms, legs and trunk continuously, you can proceed to some gentle stretching, and the accent here is on gentle. Wendy Epp, a sports physiotherapist and competitive runner and triathlete, points out that research shows you're more likely to pull a cold muscle by stretching too vigorously than by actually starting right into jogging. "It's important to warm up progressively. A low-intensity, rhythmic activity like gentle jogging, which takes your muscles through a limited range of motion, will increase muscle and body temperature gradually and thus minimize the risk of injury."

Epp offers a simple analogy. She compares muscles to Plasticine, the children's toy you can mold into different shapes. When it's cold, Plasticine is hard and brittle, so if you attack it with any degree of force, it tends to break rather than bend. Only after it has been gently kneaded and manipulated does it assume its malleable character. Your muscles respond in much the same way.

The rule with stretching, before, during and after exercise, is to listen to your body: if it hurts, you've gone too far. This is true no matter how fit you are or how fast you run. You might find it annoying to get a running injury, but just imagine how frustrated you'd feel if the

A good warm-up routine

- Walk or jog slowly for 5–10 minutes
- Stretch lightly for 3–5 minutes, concentrating on your calves, hamstrings, quadriceps, hips, low back and shoulders (see exercises on pages 156–60)

injury resulted from something you thought you were doing to avoid being injured!

An array of running-specific stretches is provided on pages 156–60. Make these stretches part of every training session. In general, runners and walkers should focus on their hamstring, calf, hip flexor and lower back muscles. Hold each stretch for about 10 seconds and repeat two to three times per muscle group.

RUNNER PROFILE

Michael

Michael, 51, has always found his running partner's insistence on warming up and cooling down an aggravation. Describing himself as a "classic Type A personality," Michael says that once his running shoes were laced up, the last thing he wanted to do was stand around wheeling his arms in the air and stretching. "Once it's time to go, I just want to go. I hate waiting."

Michael often derided his partner's passion for preparation. And then one night he awoke with one of his hamstrings locked up. "I couldn't believe the pain. I reached down and felt the muscle and it was like steel. I wanted to stretch out my leg but I couldn't. I couldn't get enough leverage on it. My wife woke up almost certain I was having a heart attack; I think I was screaming."

Luckily, his wife had been a swimmer and she knew all about cramps. She tried pulling his ankle away from his buttocks but the muscle was locked too tight. She finally rolled him onto his back and then climbed up so she could use her entire body weight to push down on his knee while at the same time using both hands to pull at his ankle. Eventually the muscle started to give and the more it stretched out, the more pliable it became, until finally Michael's leg was lying flat on the bed. "I venture to say it was the most painful thing I've ever endured; I think I would have gone insane if my wife hadn't been there," Michael recalls.

"When I told my running partner about it, he just shook his head and told me I might like to start thinking about some post-run stretching. Now I do it religiously. I still hate it, but I have only to recall that night to get on with it." Michael says that even so, the tendency for his leg to cramp has remained, a painful legacy. "Sometimes in a movie theater when there's not much leg-room, I'll start to feel it go and I'll jump up and straighten it out. I have to both stretch it and relax it to make the cramp go away. It's scary."

Cooling Down

Just as a warm-up is the best way to prepare your body for increased levels of activity, a cooling-down procedure is the best way to ease it back down to idle speed. It's a good idea to keep your muscles active for 10 to 15 minutes after exercising using a similar but less intense version of exactly the same thing you did during your warm-up. Light stretching is sufficient for your cool-down; hold each stretch for 15 to 30 seconds and repeat two to three times.

In time you'll find that the nice warm muscles you developed during your training session are more pliable, and that makes your post-exercise period a perfect time to work on your flexibility. After your training session has your muscles thoroughly warmed up, you can safely hold each stretch for anywhere from 30 seconds to 3 minutes.

Post-activity stretching serves two purposes. The most important reason you want to stretch after your training session is that muscles tighten during exercise and unless you stretch them out again, they tend to stay tight.

The other benefit to cool-down stretching is that it can help you increase the range of motion in your joints. Keep in mind that your ability to increase your range of motion is influenced by a number of things, including age, pre-existing conditions (such as old injuries) and joint structure. Try not to think of stretching as a competitive sport. Every body stretches differently and the fact that your running partner seems able to stretch further doesn't mean there's something wrong with you. Be satisfied with incremental gains and look for benefits over the long haul.

A good cool-down routine

- Walk or jog slowly for 5–10 minutes, keeping your arms moving forward and back in circles
- Stretch your hamstring and calf muscles for flexibility now that they are warm (see exercises, page 156)

Both age and gender influence flexibility in the average person. Girls are more flexible than boys and both grow less flexible after adolescence.

Some athletes argue that post-exercise stretching is the key to avoiding muscle soreness, but the case has been overstated. A certain amount of muscle soreness is natural after exercise. If you don't find yourself back to normal in about 48 hours, however, you may have injured yourself. If you think this may be the case, see a qualified sport medicine practitioner.

To sum up, begin your cool-down by walking or slowly jogging for 5 to 10 minutes. Then repeat your warm-up stretching routine, again paying special attention to

RUNNER PROFILE

Clare

Clare never thought much about running technique. She never had any aches and pains from the sport and she never ran for more than 30 minutes at a time. She did her warm-ups and stretching exercises and figured she had training licked. If there was a problem, she says, it was that she seemed to tire faster than her running partners. "We all ran the same amount of time every week and I was sure my cardio was as good as anybody's," says the 37-year-old office manager, "but at the end of the day I always seemed to be the one doing the most huffing and puffing. I don't smoke and I sleep okay, so it didn't seem to make any sense."

Although she tended to slouch, Clare never thought posture might be an issue. Then one day her running partner was massaging her neck after a training session and commented on its tightness. " 'It's always been like that,' I told him. You know how it is, you hardly notice things you've been living with for your entire life."

Her partner suggested that because she slouched a bit when she ran, the tension and fatigue might stem from some kind of problem with her running technique. Clare gave the matter more thought, and eventually asked an instructor at her gym to watch her run. He told her that when she hunched over she was tensing up, which might be contributing to the tight muscles. And because slouching could constrict the chest cavity and reduce lung capacity, it might be contributing to her fatigue. He told her to think about "running tall," to pull back her shoulders and lift her chin.

"It's not like a miracle cure or anything," Clare says, "but once I started to think about my posture and running technique, I started to think about it all the time. Now I really do think my posture is better."

stretches working your hamstrings, calves, hip flexors and lower back muscles. For cool-down only, hold each stretch about 15 to 30 seconds, repeating two to three times per muscle group. If you are working on your flexibility, hold each stretch position for anywhere from 30 seconds to 3 minutes and repeat two to three times per muscle group.

Running Techniques

When you first start running, technique will likely not be something you need worry about. Most bodies automatically adopt the technique best suited to them. (At least, they do so in the best of all possible worlds. The wrench in the works can be old injuries or hereditary misalignments. See Chapter 8, Common Injuries & Recovery.)

The amount of energy lost because of poor running technique becomes more of an issue when and if you start running longer distances. Running coach Roy Benson describes the ideal biomechanics of an elite runner as follows. "The key seems to be in watching the upper body and making sure the shoulders aren't overrotating, twisting from side to side. The arm swing should be just as comfortable as if you were walking, swinging a little bit away from you on the backside to just in front of your thigh in the front."

If you find this difficult to envisage, don't worry about your form—being relaxed is even more important. Although most people get tense when they're physically stressed, runners should avoid tension for at least two reasons. First, tight muscles may be more susceptible to injury. Second, it takes a lot of energy to stay tense; relaxing helps channel that energy into running. While you're

Stretching for flexibility

- Stretch deeply only after you are completely warmed up—after your workout—to increase or maintain your level of flexibility

Avoiding the "stitch"

- Alter your breathing pattern
- Exhale forcefully (grunt on exhalation)
- Belly breathe (breathe mainly with the diaphragm)
- Increase your abdominal strength through exercises

following the 13-week program, just try to think about relaxing, assuming good posture (open up your chest cavity by not hunching forward) and putting one foot in front of the other. If you have problems you think might be caused by poor technique, see Chapter 6, Becoming a Better Runner, where running technique is examined in more detail.

Safety First

Running on roads can make you vulnerable, especially if you are a woman. With the view that forewarned is forearmed, here are a few safety tips to make your training sessions more enjoyable—by making them safer.

- Always carry identification or write your name, phone number and blood type on a piece of paper. Put it in a running shoe key holder and attach it to the top of one of your shoes.
- Carry appropriate coins in case you need to use the phone. Keep a whistle or noisemaker in your pocket or hanging around your neck.
- Don't wear jewelry—it can attract attention you really don't want.
- Write down your running route and leave it with a friend or somewhere it can easily be found. Discuss running routes with your running friends and family.
- Run in familiar areas. Know the location of telephones and businesses or stores that are sure to be open when you run. Don't be too predictable—consider altering

your route every now and again, especially if the same person frequently shows up on your route.

- Depending on where you live, avoid running in unpopulated areas, and on deserted streets and over-grown trails. Avoid unlit areas at night. Stay clear of parked cars and bushes.

- Run against traffic so you can observe approaching vehicles. Remember, your seeing the cars does not guarantee that their drivers see you. If they're coming up behind you, you're vulnerable.

- Respect the flow of traffic. Stay out of bicycle and vehicle lanes. Move out of the way when you are being passed by cyclists or in-line skaters on shared pathways. If you are running or walking in a group, go in single file, leave room for others to get by and keep an eye open for pedestrians and small children.

- If you're running in low light or after dark, wear clothing with reflective strips. If you don't like any of the gear that comes with such strips, buy some reflective tape and put it on the clothing you do like to wear. Consider a reflective vest. Ankle reflectors designed for cyclists work just as well for runners.

- Stay alert. The more aware you are of your surroundings, the less vulnerable you are and the greater the likelihood that you will be prepared to act in an emergency. For this reason, don't wear headphones when you train. Your ears are a survival tool, a kind of 360-degree aural radar. Don't defeat their purpose.

 Running with headphones is running toward trouble. Ears are a survival device, allowing you to hear what you can't see.

- Ignore verbal harassment. Use discretion in acknowledging strangers. Look directly at people and be observant, but keep your distance and keep moving.
- Trust your intuition. Avoid any person or area that "feels" unsafe.
- Call the police immediately if something happens to you or someone else, or if you are being followed or harassed.

The Psychology of Running

RUNNERS COME TO APPRECIATE EARLY IN THEIR RUNNING careers that a fit body won't travel very far if there isn't a fit mind traveling along with it. Sometime during your training—probably on a cold, rainy, windswept day—you may find yourself staring out the window and discover that you have a remarkable capacity for making excuses. You'll be able to come up with all sorts of reasons to avoid heading out into what has suddenly become a world hostile to running. Or perhaps it's not that hostile, but you're just not in the mood. In this mind game, the solitary player is both winner and loser. You win by avoiding what you don't want to do; you lose by avoiding what you know needs to be done.

Staying on track is sometimes more difficult than initially getting to it. The 13-week walk/run program is designed to help you become a runner while exposing you to the least amount of risk, both physical and mental. However, running is work. Getting your heart rate up and covering increasing distances will make you sweat and tire you out. Your body and mind will benefit, but the action itself will be laborious. For that reason, as you progress through the program, and even later on, when you've trained yourself to be a

✓ Running with a partner or group is more motivating and increases safety, especially for women runners. Running with your dog can keep both you and your pet healthy.

runner, there may be days when you just don't feel like running. This chapter offers suggestions for dealing with those days.

Listen to Your Body

Sometimes you should listen to your body and not run. If you're sick, subjecting your body to additional stress might lead to injury or more serious illness. Your body needs its strength to recover; give it a chance. This includes times when you made yourself sick in the first place, by staying out too late, eating too much or drinking too much alcohol. (A lot of people think the best cure for a hangover is strenuous physical exercise, but this probably has more to do with a desire for self-punishment than the benefits of exercise. Avoid the problem in the first place by not overindulging.)

The same goes for running when you have a minor injury, or one that could become serious if not attended to. Some athletes are constantly nursing chronic aches and pains, yet many other athletes almost never seem to suffer

RUNNER PROFILE

Jack

Jack, a 72-year-old engineer who's currently "failing" at retirement, says getting motivated to run was no problem, especially after his first quadruple bypass operation. "I want to stay alive," he says simply. "When you've had surgery like that and you consider the alternative, it's not very hard to get motivated."

Before his surgery, Jack had started the 13-week walk/run program because his son wanted to learn to run and Jack wanted to be a supportive father. Today he runs with both his son and his daughter. "It's a communication thing now," he says. "They're busy with their families a lot of the time. When they do come over, they've got six children between them and it's kind of hard to have an adult conversation. Running gives us a chance to catch up and talk to each other as adults."

from long-term disabilities. If you ask both how they deal with injuries, you will almost invariably learn that the chronically injured ones think it's nobler to run through pain than to take a break or deal with the problem. "Ignore it long enough and it will go away," they'll often tell you.

They're nearly always wrong.

Train Your Mind

Motivation is a funny thing. You've probably found that you have more of it when you're not actually confronting whatever task you have assigned yourself. Napoleon understood this when he spoke of "the courage of the early morning." Soldiers would boast around the campfires at night, when they had some wine in their bellies, but were often less brave when the sun appeared on the horizon and the time came to march into battle. The truly brave, said Napoleon, were those whose courage did not abandon them when they strapped on their cuirasses and mounted their steeds.

The same is true for athletes. It's easy to conquer mountains or run marathons when the lights are out and you're peacefully dozing under the blankets; it's quite another when you're awake. To go from being a dreamer to being a doer, you have to train your mind the same way you train your body.

Nobody says, "I'm going to be a runner," and a month or two later jogs across the finish line at the New York Marathon. To become a runner, you train your body slowly, over an extended period. If you stick with the program in this book, you will develop a more robust cardiovascular system and a toughened musculoskeletal system, and will

Too tired to exercise?

Here are some tips for getting yourself motivated:

- Exercise early in the day
- Don't stay up late—turn off the tube and get your sleep
- Reduce your intake of high-sugar foods
- If you exercise after work, have a healthy late-afternoon snack to give you energy (e.g., a bagel, fruit or yogurt)
- Try different kinds of exercise until you find the ones you like best

be able to run for some distance without gasping for air or pulling an Achilles tendon.

Your mind, too, needs training. You don't go from thinking on Tuesday that runners are lunatics to motivating yourself to run 30 minutes on Wednesday. Train your mind the same way you train your body: moderately, consistently, and with the reward of rest for its efforts. If you do these things, your mind will serve your goals instead of sabotaging them.

Think of yourself as an athlete

Your first and most important goal for the mind is to think of yourself as an athlete. No matter how far you can run, you are an athlete. No matter what your reason for taking

RUNNER PROFILE

Chris

After 40 years of inertia, Chris found himself wondering about the state of his health as he struggled through his middle years. "It got to the point where I thought I'd better do something," recalls the 64-year-old operator of a chain of retail gift stores. "It was a little intimidating at first because I looked around at the rest of the running group and there were hardly any other guys as old as I was, but then the program started out so slowly I found I was okay."

His heightened level of fitness has had a positive effect on his marriage, he adds. Although he hasn't managed to talk his wife into taking up running, she has started in-line skating and now skates beside him as he pants his way through local parks. Motivation is a problem for him now and then, but he's already figured out that if the spirit is unwilling, the best thing to do is call up a friend and rely on the buddy system. "Some of the rainy nights can be tough, but I find the best thing is to go with other people and not try to do it by yourself. That's the whole secret for me; I always maintain that if you try to do it all yourself, you'll never make it."

Chris has had invitations to train harder and enter a half marathon, but that isn't going to happen, he says. "I'm only doing this for myself and I don't want to go any farther than 10 k. That's enough for me."

up running—whether it's weight control, overall fitness, social contacts or something else—you are an athlete. You subject yourself to regular training sessions and stress both your mind and body in pursuit of your goals, so you are, by definition, an athlete. It may seem like an exaggeration, but once you lace on a good pair of running shoes you are—if you'll pardon the pun—on an equal footing with the world's best runners. "Oh sure," you say, "like I could run with the world's best?" In fact, you can. If you were to line up at the London Marathon, for example, you'd be toe to toe with the world's premier runners, on the same surface, using the same equipment. You might lose sight of them pretty quickly and not see them again for several hours, but unlike just about any other sport, running allows recreational athletes to compete against the world's best.

The only meaningful difference between you and people who run marathons in less than three hours is that they've been training a lot longer. Of course, there are gifted athletes who make any sport look effortless, who by virtue of the bodies and hearts nature gave them are capable of amazing feats of strength and endurance. In most cases, however, their seemingly effortless performances are built upon tens of thousands of hours of hard work. And anybody can work hard, including you.

When you start to think of yourself as an athlete, you'll find it easier to be active. As most psychologists will tell you, imagining you are a certain somebody makes it a lot easier to be that somebody. You may be a recreational athlete rather than a world-class competitive athlete, but your goals and the efforts you put into achieving them differ

No time to exercise?

- Go for a brisk walk on your lunch break
- Get off the bus a few stops early and walk part of the way
- Combine activities— read on an exercise bike, socialize by walking with friends, run on the treadmill while watching TV

Morning is one of the best times to run, for several reasons. Among them: Not only is it statistically safer, but what you plan to do first in the day usually gets done.

only by degree, not kind. If you learn to respect those goals and think of the effort you put into achieving them as worthwhile, you will also increase your self-respect along the way.

Find your focus; the "fun" will come

Motivational experts will tell you that the best way to get in shape is to find something you have fun doing that also serves the goal of improving your fitness. When you first take up running, you may find the "fun" a little hard to discover. Although there is a lot to enjoy about running, fun is more a corollary than an intrinsic part of it. Some people seem to be naturally suited to running, and these people enjoy it immensely from the word go. If you're not one of them, focus on the reasons you came to running in the first place. If you wanted to improve your social life, think about all your new pals; if you sought the solitude of running, concentrate on that. If you came to improve your fitness level, think about how each step you take puts you that much closer to good health.

The really good news is that even though fun may not be the operative word when you begin to run, it certainly

RUNNER PROFILE

Donna

Donna wanted to run three days a week, but her running group met only twice a week. This presented the then 49-year-old accountant with a challenge. "Motivation seems to be a problem for me when I have to go by myself. If I say I'm going to meet you, I'll meet you, but if I don't have anybody to meet, it seems I can come up with all kinds of excuses not to run."

Donna still hasn't quite figured out how to lick her running-alone blues, but she knows she can motivate herself by seeking out running companions. "I've made a lot of new friends," she says, adding, "In that way it's really changed my life."

can be later on. By the time you have completed the 13-week walk/run program and trained yourself to run continuously for 30 minutes or more, you will find yourself having more fun. You'll come to enjoy the feeling of robustness and power in your body when your heart starts pumping. You'll be looking forward to meeting up with your running partner or group for the social contact it gives you. Or perhaps you'll look forward to getting away by yourself and thinking your own thoughts as you pound through a forest somewhere at the edge of the world.

Seek out variety

Most beginning runners start off the program all fired up with an enthusiasm founded on a series of interlocking goals. As you move through the program, you will face increasing levels of physical and mental stress, which in itself can be highly motivating. Your ability to perform the tasks at each level will also provide satisfaction. But sometimes this isn't enough.

Dr. David Cox, a clinical psychologist who has worked with a large number of sports programs in Canada, recommends that you continually seek new ways to enjoy running after becoming involved in the sport. For example, you may find running around your neighborhood sufficiently rewarding in the beginning, but over time the experience may pale—you've seen the same garbage cans and been chased by the same dogs so many times that you don't think you can stand it any more. When this happens, it's time to change your running habits. Find a different place to run. Go exploring. Run in the park or along a beach. Go running in the country. Take your dog with you. Change the time of day that you run. There's no need to let running become stale.

Run with others

Another way to spark your enthusiasm is to run with a partner or group. Running with other people not only gives you a social occasion to look forward to but makes you accountable: you are expected to appear. Joining a running group can pay off in many ways. People who join running groups are often as disparate as the creatures gathering around a jungle watering hole, but when it comes to running they are equals sharing a passion for a similar activity. Running is a great social equalizer: when you're moving down the road together, nobody cares if

Cathy

For Cathy, a 51-year-old self-employed television writer, fun was not the operative word when it came to beginning to run. She walked regularly, thanks to the addition of a dog to the family, but running had never been on her agenda. Then a friend showed her a flyer for the 13-week walk/run program and she decided to try it, partly to see if it was something she wanted to do and partly because she wanted to see if she could do it.

The first days were anything but auspicious. "The group leaders were really accepting of every fitness level, but the very first time I went out I was huffing and puffing during the first 30-second run. I felt that it would never end. One of the group leaders, a man in his 60s, came up and told me I didn't have to run if I didn't want to. He later confessed to me that he thought I was going to have a heart attack."

Cathy persevered, but although after a good year of training she now finds running enjoyable, she still finds the first 10 minutes a grind. "Running is an essential part of my daily life now and I run three to four times a week, but I never enjoy the first few minutes." She gets past her initial lack of enthusiasm by comparing her first few minutes of running to jumping into a pool. "It's hard to do at first, but once you're in, you enjoy the water. Every day I have to remind myself that once I get going I'll enjoy it."

you're a brain surgeon or a janitor, a lawyer or a coffee shop barrista. You are a brother or sister in the cause, and just as the people you run with are the impetus for you overcoming your inertia, you are what gets them going. Sometimes there are other payoffs as well, including social activities apart from running, such as brunches or dinner outings. You never know, you might even meet someone special. (Running groups are not a pick-up scene for singles, but it's not as though love has never blossomed somewhere between miles 6 and 7.)

Make running a time for you

Group running isn't for everyone. Some people find that being alone is what makes running worth all the effort. People who feel crowded between their work and home lives often resort to running because it's the only time they have to be alone with themselves. Sport psychologist David Cox believes that running after you leave work and before you arrive home at the end of the day could be one of the best things you can do for your sanity. "The literature suggests that most people who burn out need some kind of decompression between work and home, and exercise can operate as a great buffer between the two. Sometimes a run after work and before you start to interact with your family can have a really positive impact on your home life. It allows you to decompress in a safe way and is a lot healthier than going to a bar or going home and mixing a drink."

If you're bedeviled by stress, constantly worrying that your life is out of balance, a regular running program can give you an area of your life that you can truly call your

Stress-busting tips

- Exercise regularly
- Eat sensibly
- Get adequate sleep
- Don't sweat the small stuff
- Visualize something positive to calm yourself
- Learn to say "no"
- Set priorities
- Keep your cool
- Do your best and leave the rest

own, one that you can control when everything else seems tinged with madness. That feeling of control may even wash over into the rest of your life.

Keep track of your tracks

As mentioned in the previous chapter, keeping a training log can help to keep you motivated. Like running with friends, having a logbook sets up accountability: if you start out keeping notes in your logbook, you'll find it difficult to avoid your responsibilities because those blank logbook pages will be staring you in the face.

Similarly, it can help to schedule your training sessions. Suppose that you've written "Training Session" in your appointment book for 4 p.m. Wednesday. If someone phones you to propose a meeting at 4:30 on Wednesday, you can tell them you already have something on then and suggest a different time. A firm date with yourself can give you the backbone to say "no" to events that would compromise your training.

RUNNER PROFILE

Teresa

It took the birth of Teresa's second child to make her think running was something she needed to incorporate into her life. "About four weeks after the birth of my second child, I looked in the mirror and didn't like what I saw," she recalls. Now, even though she has a busy career as a nurse and two children to raise, Teresa never has any problem finding the time for her run. "There's always half an hour or an hour," she says. "You just have to make yourself get up and do it."

She has a couple of useful tricks for making it happen, too. First, she makes a point of scheduling her run into her day well in advance. "If I tell myself early in the day that that's what I'm going to do, then I usually do it." The other trick is even more cagey. "If I don't feel like going, I just put on my running gear anyway. By the time I get it on, it just makes sense to get out there and do it."

Forgive yourself

Of course there will be days when life takes over and you won't be able to do your training. You may be five weeks into the program, making great progress and feeling really good about yourself. You may be beginning to lose a little weight and starting to notice the extra energy that comes with getting fitter. Then something happens to interrupt your training. Maybe you go on a vacation, or you are under a lot of pressure at work. The bottom line is that you just can't find the time to run. Because you miss a couple of weeks, you may assume that you're back to square one.

This is not the time to lose heart. For one thing, your body is probably in better shape than you believe. Once you have gotten in shape, it takes a shorter period of time to achieve that same level of fitness again.

Even if the worst happens—you quit and have to go back to the beginning of the 13-week program and start all over—so what? People often try to stop smoking several times before they succeed; that doesn't make either the goal or the final achievement any less worthy. You may be encouraged to know that elite athletes often use a plan similar to the 13-week walk/run program to get back in shape after a serious injury. If starting back at the beginning works for them, it can work for you.

Talk to yourself—the right way

Most athletes have found that there are few opponents as formidable as their own psyche. Sport is a process of making mistakes; what matters is that participants are able to

✓ People may start an exercise program because they want to improve their health, but they will continue with it because they enjoy it.

rise above their mistakes and respect themselves enough to come back and do better the next time. As sport psychologist David Cox points out, negative self-talk tends to beget negative results. The next time you find yourself engaging in negative self-talk, ask yourself whether it has ever made you any better at what you were trying to do. If you have trouble following your training schedule, instead of berating yourself for failing, try insisting on believing that you *will* complete the 13-week walk/run program.

Use your warm-up for motivation

If you feel dozy after a long day at work, warming up can be invaluable. In addition to preparing your body for

RUNNER PROFILE

Raymond

Although he'd always thought about running, by the time he turned 60 and retired from his job, Raymond was beginning to think that the time for taking up a new sport was behind him. Nonetheless, a part of him wouldn't let go of the idea of running. "Deep down in my heart, I always thought of doing it, to see if I could." Then his wife heard about the 13-week walk/run program and Raymond decided to give it a whirl. Even though he was an active person with a passion for both golf and tennis, running presented new challenges. "It was very difficult for me at the start and there were times I didn't think I was going to be able to finish," he says.

Raymond points to two things that made it possible for him to complete the program and go on to run in a 10-k race. "One, I'm the kind of person who goes all out, so without the regimented program I probably would have tried to run too far too soon and ended up thinking running wasn't for me." And the second thing? "There were times I thought about quitting, but my wife wouldn't let me!"

Raymond runs only occasionally now—he still hears the golf courses and tennis courts calling—but he is thinking about going through the program one more time. "There's a local route where I live that has this hill," he explains. "I want to be able to say, 'Hey, I can do that.' "

exercise and preventing injuries, a warm-up can get you going psychologically, moving more oxygenated blood through your unwilling brain and spurring you on. If you really don't want to run, persuade yourself to do your warm-up anyway. By the time you're finished, you may well feel like running.

If you do manage to push yourself into doing your training when you just don't feel like it—as opposed to when your body is calling out for a necessary break (see "Listen to Your Body," on page 44)—over time you'll begin to feel good about being able to take on apathy and inertia and win. These kinds of victories feed on themselves. The more times you win, the more times you will think you can win, and the more times you think you can win, the more times you will win.

Remind yourself that it will get easier

The further you go in the training process, the easier it gets. For the first three or four months of your new athletic life, running will probably be a conscious event for your mind, just as it will be for your heart, lungs, knees and ankles. As Dr. Tim Noakes puts it, "The difficult thing is to get through that initial phase where you're thinking about your feet or your breathing or how you're never going to get through another lap and if you do it will probably kill you." But after those first months, running becomes an unconscious activity, he says, and "eventually, as the mind takes over, you stop thinking about these things. Given time, the mind will become as developed as the cardiovascular system and the musculoskeletal system."

Not only does it become easier mentally, but if you stick to the program and avoid the temptation to jump ahead, you'll go from one training level to the next with about as little physical strain as is possible in any fitness endeavor.

Hold a mental dress rehearsal

Mental rehearsal is all about imagining yourself engaged in the activity you want to have control over, as a way of preparing your mind and body for doing it.

Think about what happens when you're asleep. No doubt at some point in your life you've had a dream so vivid that it shook you into a physical response, perhaps even one so strong that it woke you up. Caught up in the

Lynn and Ken

Lynn, then 55, and her husband, Ken, then 57, discovered that running can be a great way to overcome a mid-life crisis. "Our boys are very active and running turned out to be a good way to prove to them we weren't over the hill yet," says Ken.

There were practical reasons to run as well, adds Lynn. Working in the health care field teaching exercise programs to diabetics, Lynn understands the contributions of fitness to overall health and longevity. She was the first one to tackle the program and the results astounded her. "Before, I would never have thought I could run more than a block. But soon I was running for up to 45 minutes three times a week."

Seeing the benefits enjoyed by his wife, Ken decided to lace up and try it, too. Although he was the oldest runner in his group, the graduated nature of the program allowed him to stay within his comfort zones while turning himself into a runner. Still, there were times when his enthusiasm flagged and he had to push himself a little. "When I had trouble getting out there, I gave myself a little talk: 'You don't want to lose what you've worked so hard to get,' I told myself. That usually worked."

Today, Lynn still doesn't find motivation much of a problem, largely because she enjoys the respect she's gotten from her friends and co-workers, not to mention from her 20-something sons—who've been forced to realize that it will be some time before their parents get put out to pasture.

passion of the moment, your mind was unable to separate dream from reality, and so powerful was the impulse to move that you leaped into consciousness. That same power of the mind to spur your body to action can be available to you during your waking hours. As an experiment, try to imagine yourself on your favorite running route. Start at the beginning and feel your heart rate increase and the air flowing in and out of your lungs. Imagine that you feel strong and alive and that if you wanted to, you could veer off course and run up the nearest mountain with relative ease. Now, doesn't that make you feel like running?

Break the Barriers

Life is hard; excuses are easy. Here are a few common barriers to exercise and some practical ways to overcome them.

- You're a hard-working mother and you don't want to cheat your family by taking time out for exercise.... Remind yourself that a healthy, happy mother with a positive sense of self will have more energy and patience for her family.

- You hate the way you look and you don't want other people to see your body.... Try wearing functional clothing that you feel comfortable in and perhaps even do your running somewhere private. In time you will feel better about yourself, when you begin to feel more comfortable with the exercise program.

- You work a full day in the office, you have social and family obligations on top of that, and you're too darned tired to run.... Lethargy breeds lethargy. It

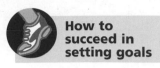

How to succeed in setting goals

- Set specific goals that can be measured
- Resist the temptation to compare yourself with others
- Set a deadline for achieving your goals
- Set challenging but realistic goals
- Set both short-term and long-term goals
- Set positive rather than negative goals
- Evaluate your progress and take time to congratulate yourself

may seem contradictory, but to get energy you have to spend energy. The more you do, the more you will be able to do.

- It's raining. It's too cold. It's too hot.... Dress for the weather and get out there.

The Family That Runs Together

CHILDREN LEARN ABOUT DIET AND EXERCISE FROM THEIR parents. Studies show that families who play together and make exercise a regular part of their lives are much more likely to have children who view exercise as an everyday practice. Regardless of whether you walk for half an hour to the park with your seven-year-old or run with your dog and baby jogger, the point is you are out-side, away from the television set—and active.

We all know that a sedentary lifestyle isn't good for us. But as many of us also know first-hand, finding the time and motivation to get active—and stay active—is not always easy. The demands of work, family and pregnancy can make it very difficult to stick with any sort of fitness program. From pregnancy and purchasing a jog-ging stroller to teaching your puppy to run with you, this chapter will give you the facts on family fitness you need to create strategies for staying active as your family grows.

Running While Pregnant

You don't have to look far to see pregnant women exercising. They are everywhere: in yoga classes, lifting weights at the local health club and jogging the trails and streets of every community. However, many women continue to ask if it's okay to run and exercise while pregnant. The short answer is, yes. According to Dr. Karen Nordahl, physician and co-author of *Fit to Deliver: Prenatal Fitness Program*, "A woman can run as long as she feels comfortable and has no pregnancy or orthopedic complications." In fact, women who were reg-

RUNNER PROFILE

Rachel

After the first few months of her pregnancy, Rachel's morning sickness subsided, and her doctor told her she could resume running—as long as she didn't overdo it. Her doctor knew that the 36-year-old is not a regular runner: she is extremely fit. In addition to her five weekly runs, she enjoys yoga and weight training. As a police officer, staying strong and in shape is essential for Rachel. She also uses running to cope with the stresses of her job and cherishes the time with her running friends.

Rachel's doctor suggested that she use the talk test as a way of monitoring the intensity level of her workouts. If she had difficulty carrying on a conversation, she needed to back off. "At first I wasn't sure if I was going to harm my baby," says Rachel, "but after getting the green light from my doctor I was happy to return to running. I've been a regular runner for years and was starting to miss not only the benefits of exercise but also my running group."

Still, in the later stages of her second trimester, "My growing stomach and extra weight made me feel less agile, and it felt as though I constantly had to go to the bathroom," says Rachel. So I decided to slow down and run shorter distances. I also made certain there were public washrooms along my running route." Even though she found it a little tedious to factor in bathroom breaks, it was worth the hassle.

Rachel ran until two weeks before she delivered a healthy baby boy. When discussing her speedy two-hour delivery of baby Caeden, Rachel jokes that she's lucky she didn't have him en route or in the coffee shop parking lot. It's hard to say if her extremely short delivery time was due to luck or her fitness level, but it was certainly a key factor in her quick recovery. "I was able to bounce back pretty quickly."

After Caeden was born, Rachel took about a month off before she resumed running. Her doctor told her she could start back sooner, but she felt it was important to listen to her body and give herself the rest she felt she needed. When she did return to running, she started slowly and took the time to build up to her pre-pregnancy running program.

ular runners before becoming pregnant usually find they can run long into their pregnancy, and for some, right up until delivery."

If you weren't a runner before you became pregnant, however, now is not the time to start running. Instead, try walking, stretching or a prenatal exercise class at your local community center.

In Dr. Nordahl's *Fit to Deliver,* she discusses the importance of a prenatal fitness program for both mom and baby. According to Nordahl's studies, a fitness regimen for expecting moms usually translates into strong, healthy mothers who have more comfortable pregnancies and an easier time in the delivery room than their more sedentary counterparts. The benefits are far reaching, from reduced rates of pregnancy-related diabetes and high blood pressure to fewer C-section deliveries and shorter labors. Furthermore, tests show that infants born to exercising moms develop motor and language skills earlier—and more effectively—than their playmates.

Nutrition tips for pre and postnatal women

Registered sport dietitian Dallas Parsons says that "overall, the recommendations for healthy eating for the general public are the same for pregnant or lactating women." Here are some of her suggestions:

- Emphasize whole grains and cereals, plenty of brightly colored fruits and vegetables, low-fat dairy or dairy alternatives and lean meats, fish, poultry or other protein sources.
- Women need 3–4 servings of dairy or other fortified dairy alternatives per day (1 serving = 1 glass of milk or other fortified beverage, $\frac{3}{4}$ cup/150 mL yogurt or $\frac{3}{4}$ oz/50 g cheese).

- Daily, choose good dietary sources of iron: meat, poultry, fish, cream of wheat, enriched breads and cereals, fortified tofu, white and kidney beans, spinach and oysters.
- Eat a meal or snack every two to three hours.
- Snacks should be foods that fit into one of the four food groups.

Jen

Jen is 35 and the mother of two. She attends regular yoga classes, runs a couple of times a week and walks a lot with her young children, both of whom were C-section deliveries.

Having a C-section delivery, according to Jen, "made it really difficult for me to return to my normal, active lifestyle. My doctor suggested it would take six weeks before I would be able to resume any kind of exercise program, but for me, it took much longer."

After the birth of her second child, Jen stayed in the hospital for four days. She would have preferred to stay longer so she could rest and have time to recover, but she was anxious to return home to her two-year-old, Lucy. For Jen, and other women, the first few weeks after a C-section delivery are pretty rough. As Jen says, she was limited as to the things she could do. She was in bed for most of the first week, and when she did walk, it was more like a shuffle. Stairs and strenuous walking were prohibited, and she experienced a lot of pain at the incision site—beyond the regular bruising. It didn't help that she developed an infection from the surgery that delayed her recovery by at least two weeks.

After six weeks, Jen was moving around comfortably. If she had wanted to, she could have started with some light jogging. But she decided to wait for a few months before going back to her regular yoga class. "Yoga was a great activity for me after my C-section. Physically I was ready to exercise, but psychologically I felt vulnerable. I was worried about my incision for a long time afterward. Still, the stretching and physical demands of yoga were great."

Jen is now expecting her third child, and another C-section delivery. She's staying fit with a bit of yoga, walking and some light jogging. Her plan after this baby arrives is to return to yoga sooner than two months after delivery because, in retrospect, she believes the classes helped in her overall recovery.

- Drink at least six glasses of fluids, including water, per day (you want to have urine that is pale in color). Proper hydration is especially important for exercising women during pregnancy, and while breast feeding, to ensure that milk supply is maintained.

- During the first trimester, women who are not exercising need approximately 100 additional calories per day (the equivalent of one extra snack). During the second and third trimesters, women need an additional 300 calories per day (the equivalent of two additional snacks or slightly larger portions at meals). If a woman is running, she will need to take in even more calories, depending on exercise duration and exertion level.

- It is recommended that women listen to their bodies and allow appetite to guide food intake. This means making healthy food choices as often as possible and listening to internal hunger cues (avoid being influenced by external stimuli, such as social pressure).

Words of caution for pregnant runners

While most women are able to exercise regularly while pregnant with few problems, it's still important to run smart:

- If you are a non-runner who is now pregnant, this is not the time to take up running. Instead, try other activities such as walking, swimming or prenatal yoga classes—discussed later in this chapter. These options will be less of a shock to your changing body.

- Monitor any pelvic or abdominal discomfort. If you experience such pains or if you are spotting after running or high-impact activities, speak with your doctor as soon as possible.

Expecting moms exercise to

- Improve energy levels
- Fight postnatal depression
- Prepare for the stress of delivery
- Improve sleep
- Reduce the chance of gestational diabetes and pregnancy-induced hypertension
- Maintain healthy weight gain
- Help oxygenate the blood (which improves energy levels)
- Promote muscle tone (which helps in the delivery process)
- Reduce common complaints such as leg cramps and constipation
- Lower blood pressure

- If running is too uncomfortable, try walking, swimming or pool running. These are great activities that put less stress on the body and joints yet still provide the benefits of exercise.

- Use common sense: avoid exercising in environments that are overly hot or humid, and avoid even mild dehydration.

- Make sure you're not working too hard, by using the talk test. If you find it difficult to speak you are pushing yourself too much. If this is the case, stop and take a break until your breathing rate is normal again and you can easily converse.

- Physicians no longer suggest that pregnant women check for maximum pulse rates during exercise. There is no evidence that it is necessary to restrict exercise when your pulse rate reaches some predetermined level.

- During the later stages of pregnancy, most women feel a "shift" in their center of gravity. This means your bal-

RUNNER PROFILE

Lacey

Lacey is a 35-year-old scientist and mother of two who ran for the first six months of both her pregnancies.

"I'm not a fast runner, but it is something that I really enjoy doing a few times a week. Still, I found that once I hit the six-month mark, it was too awkward. I was concerned about tripping. And I was running so slowly that I might as well have been walking." Lacey made the decision to switch to speed walking and attend pre- and post-natal exercise classes at her local community center. She found these classes a great way to stay fit and meet other moms.

Lacey breast-fed both children for about 18 months. "My neighbor also runs, so we would take turns looking after each other's children while the other mom went for a run. And while breast-feeding, I made sure I fed my baby first. It was never a concern." Because she exercised soon after both pregnancies, her children did not shy away from post-exercise breast milk. "Some mothers tell me their babies are fussy when breast-feeding, but I never found that to be the case."

ance is reduced. If you find running uncomfortable at this point, it's time to stop and try something else. If you are able to run up until delivery, avoid bumpy terrain and stick to flat surfaces.

Besides running, what can I do to stay fit?

As physiotherapist Denise Morbey says, "It's important for all expecting mothers to listen to their bodies. For some women, regardless of fitness level, running during pregnancy is just too uncomfortable. For others, their doctors have advised against it for health reasons. But don't become frustrated. Think of this as a time to try new activities. Cross training can help maintain total body fitness until you resume your regular running routine. Remember, this isn't the time to be concerned with improving your fitness. Staying active and healthy are better goals. Here are some ideas:

Swimming
- a great non-impact workout
- assists in maintaining aerobic fitness, upper body strength, muscle endurance and breath control

Yoga
- maintains energy, strength and flexibility
- uses static stretches, movement, breathing and relaxation techniques
- the many type of classes ensure a variety of workouts
- having fellow participants and an instructor provides support and networking

Lifestyle activities
Everyday activities can also increase your energy level, and short bouts of daily activity may fit more easily into a busy

Tips for breast-feeding moms

- Find a proper sports bra at a good running store. Today, there are many styles and sizes to meet the needs of every woman.

- Be sure to breast-feed or leave expressed milk before going for a run. This lightens your breast tissue and makes running more comfortable. Also, the baby will be full and happy during your run.

- Some reports suggest that breast milk after running has increased levels of lactic acid, which may alter the taste. But many lactating moms say this is not a problem.

- Take a water bottle and stay properly hydrated— essential for nursing mothers. Signs of dehydration include dark-colored urine and dry lips, mouth and skin.

schedule than some cross-training activities. Here are a few examples:

- gardening, raking leaves and mowing the lawn
- housework, such as cleaning, vacuuming, dusting and dishwashing
- using the stairs and walking whenever possible rather than taking elevators, escalators and moving walks
- walking during lunch breaks at work

After the Baby Arrives

After the baby arrives, women can resume running as soon as they feel able. Health care providers generally recommend waiting approximately two weeks after a vaginal birth and six to eight weeks after a Cesarean delivery. Still, it's important to check with your health care provider before resuming your exercise program. Before running, you may also want to try some fast walking. Moms should be able to walk at a good pace for approximately one hour before attempting a walk/run program. The gradual and conservative approach to exercise found in the 13-week walk/run program in Chapter 9 allows you to return slowly to running, with less of the impact time involved in continuous running.

As during pregnancy, it's particularly important for women to remain well-hydrated, especially if they're breast-feeding. "If your vaginal flow increases substantially after your workout, you have overdone it and should reduce your intensity by 10 per cent for your next workout," says Dr. Karen Nordahl. You'll also find that your breast size has increased, especially if you are breast-feeding. Finding a good sports bra is key (see page 71).

Besides increased breast size, women generally find that their pelvic floor muscles are now weak. "This can result in urinary incontinence and leakage while running, making it important for all women to strengthen these muscle groups post-pregnancy. It is particularly useful to include both core exercises and Kegels," says Dr. Nordahl.

Kegels

Named after the doctor who developed them, Kegels exercise the pelvic floor muscles that are attached to the pelvic bone—which act like a hammock to hold your pelvic organs in place. (To isolate these muscles, try stopping and starting your urine flow.) Dr. Nordahl and physiotherapist Denise Morbey suggest repeating 10 slow Kegel exercises throughout the day *after* urination (to avoid urinary retention and possible bladder infection).

Core excercises

The core muscles of the body include those of the trunk and pelvis, which are responsible for maintaining posture. During pregnancy and delivery, your core muscles have tremendous demands placed on them. By strengthening these muscles, you will be better able to support your lower back and pelvic region once you return to running.

A strong core, or midsection, assists walkers and runners in maintaining proper technique. Core strength is not about having a visible six-pack or flat stomach—it's about strengthening your midsection. For best results, consult with a strength and conditioning specialist who can assist you in setting up a program that incorporates core exercises into your training.

Choosing the right stroller

For many active parents, purchasing the appropriate baby jogger or stroller is key to maintaining or resuming their fitness regimes. Your child will use the stroller from infancy until he or she can walk a good distance, which is usually around three years of age. But with so many choices, how do you know which stroller to buy?

RUNNER PROFILE

Suzy

Suzy is a 33-year-old single mother and teacher who loves to be active. Besides running a few times a week, she has participated in numerous triathlons and tries to walk most places. When she was making the decision to have a child on her own, she knew that maintaining an active lifestyle was essential to her health and happiness. While swimming and biking would have to be put on hold for a while, she was confident that running and walking could still be done with a young baby.

A month after Lilly was born, Suzy's close girlfriends and mother gave her a large baby shower. One of the big gifts was a jogging stroller. After consulting with her doctor, however, Suzy decided to wait until Lilly was six months old before she did anything more rigorous than walk with her. Once she was half a year old, she placed her in the stroller and set out for a 45-minute run. But she returned home feeling exhausted and disappointed. She had found the stroller heavy and difficult to maneuver. She also had to walk up all of the hills, and Lilly was fussy for most of the workout. Suzy was frustrated and wondered if the jogging stroller was not going to work for her.

A friend, another mom who also runs, told Suzy that her expectations might be too high. She suggested that Suzy's fitness level had likely decreased during pregnancy, making her 45-minute-run goal too difficult. Her girlfriend suggested that, until she was more comfortable running with the stroller, she stick to flat terrain with minimal turns and bumps. Initially, Suzy was reluctant to adjust her goals, but after a couple of days she found a flat course along the ocean that looked perfect. Suzy still had problems with Lilly crying in the stroller, but, because she wasn't overtaxing herself, she had more patience and energy to deal with a fussy baby. After a month of walk/jogging, Suzy was able to run slowly for 30 minutes, and Lilly had grown more comfortable being in the stroller and only cried when she was hungry.

First, consider your needs:

- If you will mostly be walking with your child in an urban setting, it's important to choose a stroller that is easy to maneuver over curbs and down the narrow aisles of the shopping market. A lightweight stroller that is relatively inexpensive is likely your best choice.
- If you plan to run with your baby or take her/him on hikes over rough terrain, spending the extra money on a rugged jogging stroller may be a good option.
- Try out a few jogging strollers to find the one that's right for both you and your partner. Each stroller feels different. Some corner better than others, for example.
- Jogging strollers vary in height, length and seat size. If you or your partner is taller than average, your child will probably be above average in size. In this situation, you may want to choose a larger and longer stroller.

When is it safe for a baby to go in a stroller?

Before placing a baby in a jogging stroller, most health care professionals recommend waiting until she/he develops some neck strength, which is usually at around six months. At first you can help support your child's head by running on pavement rather than trails. But you don't have to wait six months to take your baby for a leisurely walk.

Walking a few weeks after the birth of a baby is a great way to get fresh air and enjoy a change of scenery from a world that has likely been limited by diapers and feedings. Walking is also good for the health and well-being of your baby. As physiotherapist Denise Morbey says, "Children

Jogging strollers

- Try out a few models
- Make sure there's a sturdy seat belt that wraps around your baby's waist and between his/her legs
- Shoulder straps are essential
- The hand brakes should easily and effectively grip the tires
- Make sure the stroller does not collapse too easily; it should have an easy-to-use locking mechanism and be easy to maneuver in a straight line
- The handle height should be waist-level or slightly below
- An adjustable canopy is essential; for rainy climates, a removable rain cover is also important

model what they see their parents doing, and it's never too early to start being good role models." You don't need to go out and train to run a 10-k race immediately following the birth of your child, but a regular walking or running program will help your youngster adopt healthy lifestyle habits.

Tips for running with baby

Wait until your baby is at least six months old before you run together. Babies need to be able to hold their head upright before they can endure the bouncing of a jogging stroller. Remember:

- It's okay to walk with your newborn to six-month-old in a stroller, but avoid rough terrain. Again, your baby does not have the strength to support his/her head and is susceptible to neck injuries.
- When first running or walking with a stroller, go easy and stick to a paved pathway or sidewalk with few bumps and turns. It takes some time to get the hang of pushing the extra weight.
- If you are new to running, try to find a short route in your neighborhood so that if you grow tired you can easily and quickly return home. If you have the energy, you can always do two loops!
- Make sure you bring extra water and a snack. Regardless of your fitness level, pushing a stroller is hard work.
- If you're a dad, or a mom who isn't nursing, think about bringing a bottle in case your baby becomes hungry while you're out on your run. It can be a long—and loud—trip home with a crying baby.

- Run with a weather-appropriate cover for the stroller. Today, any good-quality jogging stroller comes with numerous covers that meet almost all weather conditions and which are easy to remove.

Clothing for Pregnant and Nursing Runners

Pregnant women today have a great selection of maternity clothing and exercise gear to choose from, including running tights, shorts and tops designed to accommodate a changing body. Phil Moore, owner of Vancouver's LadySport running store, says, "Many pregnant women are now wearing tights that are cut in such a way that they sit below the belly. Some women simply wear a low-rise fold-over waistband tight, which is then useful after the pregnancy. My customers often find the newer designs to be more comfortable and fashionable than the traditional panel pants for the expanding waistline." He also notes that though the more conservative maternity styles are still available in most stores, Danskin, Moving Comfort, InSport and Brooks all provide maternity clothes that both feel and look great.

Even so, if you ask any nursing mother who runs, finding a sports bra that provides comfort and function while minimizing movement can still be a challenge. Some women find that because of the extra sensitivity and density of their breasts they prefer a bra that eliminates all or most movement in the breast area. Some women find wearing two bras helpful. But at least there are many choices out there. Most bra and sportswear manufacturers design an array of exercise bras to meet the needs of all women, regardless of shape and size. "There are bras built into tank tops now that are sporty and modified for feeding," says Moore. Nike and Champion Sports Bras, for example, offer good choices. They also use synthetic moisture wicking fibers so that women stay dry and warmer in winter and cooler in the summer."

The right running shoe is an equally important piece of exercise gear for pregnant and nursing moms. Given that your weight will increase and your balance decrease, it's essential to purchase a pair of shoes that meet your changing needs. (Keep in mind that when your weight increases, so does your shoe size. Your feet may "spread" and

RUNNER PROFILE

Dale

Dale is a 40-year-old father who has been running three times a week for more than 10 years. Before the arrival of his son, Kai, he and his wife, Cindy, agreed that maintaining an active lifestyle as a family was important to them. Dale and his wife rarely run together, however. She is an elite runner and often trains alone or with her running group. Yet even though Dale runs at a slower pace, it was decided that both mom and dad would take Kai on their runs.

Finding a stroller that worked for both of them took a little time. Dale is tall with a strong build, while Cindy is shorter with a slight frame. In the end, they purchased a lightweight stroller with an adjustable handle that is adaptable to both their heights.

Dale has been running regularly with Kai for almost two years now, and says that it only took a few runs for him to feel comfortable pushing the stroller. In fact, the stroller has forced him to reduce his speed, allowing him to run for longer periods at a relaxed pace. He really enjoys running with the stroller for this reason. Before, he struggled with his pacing and would often run too fast, which forced him to cut short his runs. The one thing that Dale has found a little difficult is adapting the natural swinging motion of his arms. Now when running, he pushes the stroller with one hand, which leaves the other free to move naturally. He then switches hands.

As for Cindy, she prefers to use two hands when pushing Kai. She also feels relaxed and comfortable having her baby along for the ride and, like Dale, finds the stroller easy to maneuver, even on trails.

your arches fall.) All running shoe manufacturers make shoes especially designed for the female foot, and many of these designs come in various widths to meet the needs of the thinnest and widest feet. Ask at your local running store for advice on the shoes that will best meet your needs.

Commonly Asked Prenatal and Postnatal Questions

Q: *What do I do about my increasing breast size?*
A: According to physiotherapist Denise Morbey, "breast size increases during pregnancy and even more so afterward, when breast-feeding." Morbey recommends that pregnant runners wear proper-fitting sports bras, and notes that those with a T-back shoulder strap increase directional support.

Q: *My feet are growing. Why is this happening?*
A: Increased weight means increased stress on the feet, so pregnant women need to pay attention to footwear. Shoes tend to break down sooner so it's important to replace old runners. If you're unsure about the support your shoes are providing, check with a footwear specialist at your local running store.

Q: *My balance is terrible now that I'm pregnant. What can I do to improve this?*
A: "With increased weight gain in the abdomen," says Dr. Karen Nordahl, "a woman's center of gravity shifts. But although balance is more of a concern, it's not necessarily a limitation for runners." One suggestion is to try balance training: yoga, or just standing on one leg and alternating, are just two of the ways you can do this. As well, avoid trails with rocks and roots in order to minimize the risk of falling.

Running _en famille_

- Be willing to alter your workout to run with your little one in a stroller or baby jogger
- Encourage your kids to rollerblade or ride a bike or scooter alongside you
- Ask your partner to ride a bike or run with you sometimes
- If the kids are too young to go far, head for the nearest playground, then do your workout around them while they play
- Try a "destination" run—to the nearest ice-cream shop; a picnic after your run together is another incentive for kids

—*Olympian Lynn Kanuka*

Q: *I'm pregnant and concerned about running because of the loosening of soft tissues. What should I do?*

A: Soft tissues loosen with pregnancy, though as Dr. Nordahl points out, "running helps maintain a strong pelvic floor and stabilizers." Still, it's important for pregnant runners to be aware of their bodies. "Women should stop running if they experience any pelvic pain when standing or landing on one leg." If you don't stop, says Nordahl, "this can cause shearing of the sacroiliac joint." Pain may also occur in the belly due to the ligaments being overstressed during the impact of running. And soreness in the knees, hip joints, low back and feet should not be ignored. If you are suffering from any of these problems, consult your physician and discuss eliminating the stress of running on land in favor of pool running.

Q: *I had an episiotomy and want to return to running. What should I do?*

A: "The scar from an episiotomy, like any soft-tissue scar," says Morbey, "requires appropriate time to heal." She recommends waiting at least eight weeks before resuming a running program, though this can vary depending on the individual. More time may be needed if there has been an infection or the healing rate is slow. Once healed, the episiotomy scar should not be a hindrance while running.

Q: *I had a C-section delivery. Will this affect my return to running?*

A: According to Dr. Nordahl, "A C-section will delay a woman's return to her running program. A Cesarean section is considered major surgery, so it's important to give the body time to heal. The fatigue associated with caring for a newborn may also delay resumption of exercise."

Guidelines for Children Who Want to Run

It is impractical to make general rules and guidelines regarding acceptable distances that children should run. This is because children grow and mature at different rates, making it next to impossible to lump them physiologically or skeletally into general groups between birth and adolescence. As a result, guidelines and rules for children wanting to train for road races, track-and-field and cross-country events need to be reasonable and based on the abilities of the individual child.

As pediatrician Dr. Trent Smith says, "Expectations need to be flexible. It's also important to take into consideration the child's level of activity prior to commencing running. The more active a child is early on, the more they will be able to do at the start of a running program."

It is best to use common sense when planning a running program for pre-adolescents. The Canadian Paediatric Society says there are no clear running guidelines for this group of runners. Dr. Smith suggests that running a 10-k race may be too much for most children, but a Grade 5 or 6 student who has run a couple of 5-k races could likely run a 10-k race with some training.

How should kids train?

Children who want to complete a 5- or 10-k race need to train the same way adults do when they are attempting these goals. But to hold a child's interest, parents and teachers need to keep training fun. By making exercise play-driven, kids are more likely to be inspired and want to exercise every day. If kids see running only as hard

Is your child a runner?

- Make sure your child has appropriate running shoes
- The running program should be child-driven *not* parent-driven—kids need to have fun
- Children should not run every day; every other day is best
- If your child complains of pain, visit a sport medicine practitioner
- Children need to drink water every 10–15 minutes when exercising
- Watch the temperature carefully: your child is more susceptible to extreme temperatures (both hot and cold) than you are and needs to be dressed appropriately

work, it is unlikely they will want to exercise into their teen and adult lives.

Making running fun for kids

If your child expresses interest in joining you on a run or walk, encourage him/her to accompany you on a bike. After watching you run, your child may catch the running bug and want to run as well.

If this is the case, consider exploring local trails, and modify the walk/run program. Have your child run to specific landmarks along the trail, such as a log or a tree— then wait for mom or dad to catch up. Walk to another landmark before your child runs again. If you don't have easy access to trails, this type of run can be done around your neighborhood: your child can run to the end of the block, for example, or along the schoolyard fence. Always keep in mind that most kids don't enjoy running the same way adults do. By making it fun, they'll see their time on the trails as a game rather than a training session.

Running with the Family Dog

Dogs are one of the best motivators to get us off the couch and on the road to improved health and fitness. You'd be hard-pressed to find more energetic and committed run-

Jackie

Jackie is a 45-year-old elite runner who runs competitively and trains most days. Cozi, her new husky puppy, will soon be her number one training partner. "Sure I enjoy training with my running friends, but running with a dog is different. It's great. You don't have to talk or listen, you can just run, knowing that this little friend is just as happy to be out on the trails as you are. Quiet and content to be along for the ride... there is nothing better!"

ning partners. Fit dogs also have more energy, sleep better and are more aware of their surroundings.

Of course, like humans, all dogs are not created equal. Some breeds, or builds, are better suited for running than others. A good running dog has a medium build, weighs 50 to 70 pounds (22.5 to 31.5 kilograms) and has short to medium-short hair. Evidence suggests that retired greyhounds, Labradors, retrievers, setters, spaniels and working dogs such as border collies and huskies make good running dogs. Cross breeds can also make great running companions. Less suitable breeds for running include large dogs such as Great Danes as well as small dogs such as Chihuahuas, because of their short legs. Flat-faced dogs such as pugs and boxers also find running a challenge, because of their difficulty breathing.

Getting started

The general rule is that dog owners should wait until their dog is fully grown before running together. With smaller dogs, this means waiting until your pup is at least six months old; with larger dogs you can begin when your dog is about one year old.

If you are a regular runner and plan to have your dog accompany you on most training runs, it's a good idea to have your pet checked by a vet to ensure there are no lung, heart or joint problems and that your dog is up to the challenge of a distance running program.

It may seem like dogs are made to run, because they are enthusiastic and rarely refuse an offer to run with their owner. But the repetitive pounding, pace and duration of a run can be difficult and harmful for some dogs.

Running without stopping is unnatural for a dog. They are pack animals, with a natural tendency to push hard in order to keep up.

Most veterinarians and dog trainers suggest that dogs should not run longer than 3 miles (5 kilometers). A dog may display energy and enthusiasm to run great distances, but it is important to be cautious and conservative when planning the distance and duration of your runs when training with a pet.

Make a running plan for your pooch, even if it's a running breed. The plan should include a gradual buildup in time and distance over several weeks. This way, your dog's endurance will improve over time, limiting the aches and pains commonly associated with an overly aggressive schedule.

Some of the warning signs that a dog has done too much include increased saliva, vomiting, irregular breathing and an uneven gait. If you notice these signs, have your dog stop and take a break. If the symptoms persist, take your pet to the vet to be checked out.

Becoming a Better Runner

YOU'RE RUNNING, AND YOU LIKE IT AND WOULD LIKE TO GET even better at it. Near the end of this chapter, we offer some advice on improving your running technique. But there are a number of other things you can do to become a better athlete and improve your overall fitness, all of which will also make you a better runner. Among your options are cross training (which in itself offers many options), strength training and stretching.

Cross Training

Cross training means participating in a variety of training activities. Almost any activity that gets you huffing and puffing qualifies: skiing (both cross-country and downhill), cycling, swimming, in-line skating, ice skating, hiking, walking, climbing, circuit training and aerobic exercise to music are all excellent choices. By taking part in one of these activities in addition to running, you can increase your overall fitness and build strength in general instead of in areas specific only to running.

The benefits of cross training include resting certain muscle groups while using different ones. Cross training also helps athletes avoid boredom. The variety of different exercises can be a psychological boost.

Cross training will also reduce your risk of injury. Following the 13-week walk/run program will give your body, from your heart to your Achilles tendons, the best possible chance to adjust to the stresses and strains of running. There would be no need for such a program if the stresses and strains weren't there. But running *can* be

RUNNER PROFILE

Lynda

If the most dedicated anti-smokers are former smokers, the most dedicated runners are probably people who previously thought runners were out of their minds. Lynda is a case in point. "Before I did the 13-week training program, I thought running was one of the stupidest things on the face of the earth. How could anyone possibly enjoy it?"

Still, the same way many smokers wake up one day and want to butt out, when the then 41-year-old office worker was diagnosed with a blood-pressure problem, she decided some things in her life had to change. She heard that the 13-week walk/run program was one way to ease into fitness and decided to try it. When she sprained an ankle (because of wearing poor shoes) halfway through the program, she temporarily changed over to cycling; later, she completed the program just in time to run an 8-k race in 50 minutes. She then trained for a half marathon, and her training schedule had her right on pace.

"On Tuesdays and Thursdays, I ran for half an hour and then did weights, both the universal gym and free weights. I'd go for light weights and lots of reps; I never bench pressed more than 20 pounds (9 kilograms). I started doing it because I was told you can't improve your speed unless you improve your strength." Wednesdays, Lynda alternated between finding a hill and doing speed drills. With the hill training, she started out with 5 reps up the hill and increased it by one climb each session. On the intervening Wednesdays, her speed drill consisted of alternately running flat out for 1 minute and jogging for 1 minute. She started out running 1 minute flat out, followed by 1 minute of jogging (recovery)—repeated 5 times. Her goal was to work up to 12 repetitions, for both her speed training and hill climbing. "On Saturdays she ran with a group for 40 to 60 minutes and on Sundays she did an endurance run."

hard on your body, especially if you were born with some biomechanical imbalances (high arches, for instance, or a misaligned kneecap), or if you have ever been injured. Participating in other aerobic activities serves many of the same goals as running—producing good cardiovascular fitness in addition to increased strength, endurance and weight control—but shifts the stress around, so that it isn't all borne by the same parts of the body. With some sports—notably cycling, swimming, in-line skating and cross-country skiing—the musculoskeletal stress is quite low. Thus by cross training, you'll get stronger, you'll be fitter and you'll also give your ankles, knees and hips a break from the pounding action of running.

Cross training strengthens the body and can actually make you a better runner than if you train just by running. Dr. Tim Noakes says that if he had his running career to do over, he would compete in more triathlons. "Marathons and ultra-marathons [50 miles/80 kilometers and up] are what really wear you out."

Cycling is one of the cross-training activities most commonly favored by runners. Cycling strengthens primarily your quadriceps (the big muscle group at the front of your upper leg), whereas running uses primarily the hamstrings (the big muscle group at the back of your upper leg). Developing balanced strength in "opposing" muscle combinations such as the quadriceps and hamstrings (see "Strength Training," page 158) is an important way to avoid injury.

Another activity runners often choose is cross-country skiing, because it's a huge aerobic challenge and works

Passive exercise devices—rolling machines, vibrating belts, vibrating tables and motor-driven bicycles and rowing machines—will not break up fat or help you shed weight. Massage will improve circulation and induce relaxation, but it will not change your shape.

Pool running can be far less tedious than swimming laps.

- Do it with a friend— you can talk like you're on a jog
- To pass the time, alternate slow and fast efforts
- Pick a pool with good tunes—and run to the music

—*Olympian Lynn Kanuka*

virtually every muscle in the body, both upper and lower. Of course, your opportunities to ski will be limited by the climate in which you live.

Pool running, which can be done in any climate, is gaining in popularity. Basically, you just jog in deep water while wearing a flotation device. Pool running is usually practiced only by the very dedicated and by people recovering from injuries.

Another advocate of cross training is Mark Spitz, the American swimmer who dominated men's swimming in 1972, bringing home a treasure-trove of medals (seven of them gold) from that year's Summer Olympics. Spitz says the reason swimmers today are beating his times by very large margins is that they're not spending all their time in the pool; rather, they're cross training and strengthening their bodies in other ways. Similarly, at the recreational as well as the competitive level, cross training can actually make you a better, stronger runner than if you train just by running.

Another benefit of cross training is that in exploring its options, you may well discover another sport you really like. When you do, you can help your body adjust to its rigors by applying principles similar to those you learned in the 13-week program.

If you are taking up exercise at least in part as a way of controlling your weight, you will want to know how other activities stack up against running in terms of energy requirements. The following list shows a variety of activities, from less to more strenuous. As the list indicates, running at a fast pace (7 minutes per mile/4.5 minutes per kilometer) is more effective in burning calories.

Volleyball (recreational)	
Cycling (leisurely pace)	**less**
Table tennis (recreational)	**strenuous**
Walking (moderate pace)	
Circuit training with free weights	
Aerobics (medium intensity)	
Swimming (slow crawl)	
Running (11½ min/mi or 7 min/km)	
Aerobics (intense)	
Swimming (breast stroke, intense pace)	
Cycling (racing)	
Racquetball	
Running (9 min/mi or 5.5 min/km)	
Squash	
Running (7 min/mi or 4.5 min/km)	**more**
	strenuous

Finally, cross training helps you avoid the biggest enemy of all training programs: psychological burnout. It allows you to work at improving your fitness level without subjecting you to the same routine day after day, keeping you from getting bored.

In brief, cross training can:

• distribute the load of training among various body parts, thereby reducing the risk of injury;

• add variety to your workouts to keep you from losing interest;

• allow you to continue training if you are injured, by using uninjured joints and muscles in a different activity;

- develop your entire body, rather than only a few specific parts.

More facts about some specific cross-training activities, along with some of the reasons you might want to consider incorporating them into your life, appear below. Keep in mind, however, that you needn't limit yourself to just these activities. Table tennis isn't included, but besides being a lot of fun to play, it's a great game for working up a sweat and developing hand-eye coordination. No matter what activity you choose, remember to heed the three rules of training: moderation, consistency and rest.

Swimming

Swimming provides a non-impact workout, which makes it a superior choice if you are injured. It will assist in boosting your aerobic fitness, upper body strength, muscular endurance and breathing control. This last feature is especially valuable. Your muscles need a steady supply of

Liz

Liz, 41, has three kids, is vice-president of a high-tech firm and spends a good deal of her time "flying all over the world." When she was 36, she also wanted to complete a triathlon. "I would have done it that summer but I had a hernia operation and that held me back. Nothing to do with running," she quickly adds, laughing. "It was the kids."

Being so busy, her solution to finding the time to keep fit was to hire a personal trainer. Although Liz found it difficult to schedule her week too far in advance, she dealt with the inconsistencies by working with someone who could drop everything and come running when she was needed, usually three times a week. It cost money, but Liz believes the money was well spent. "I need a lot of energy to do all the things I have to do in a day and keeping fit is the only way to get it. My trainer had a really good program of weight training, cardiovascular activities and stretching.

oxygen, and although you don't want to breathe too deeply or too fast, because you can hyperventilate and make yourself dizzy, too little air will leave you breathless. Swimming teaches you to breathe rhythmically. It isn't very expensive and can be done year-round, both indoors and out.

It is important to keep in mind that swimming is not ideal for weight loss: water supports so much of the body that swimming doesn't burn as many calories per minute as running does.

Cycling

There used to be two types of road warriors in this world, those who ran and those who rode, but the benefits of cross training are making for a lot of crossover. Both groups are finding that the other sport complements their own and leads to a better degree of overall fitness.

As mentioned in the general information on cross training, cycling enhances muscle balance between the hamstrings and the quadriceps, which can help prevent injuries on the weaker side. Cycling also provides a good workout for your legs with less pounding and jarring than running.

Cycling can be a lot of fun, too. You can cover vast distances with less effort, and explore new neighborhoods and trails. Mountain bikes have an advantage over road bikes in that they allow you to get off roads you are forced to share with automobiles. Depending on how extreme you get, trail riding can be a very intense workout. Off-road riding doesn't require a costly top-of-the-line bike, just one strong enough to take the bumps.

 The average woman has less muscle mass than the average man, and thus typically has about 60 to 85 per cent of the absolute strength of a man.

There are no magic pills or special elixirs that can improve your running performance significantly. Improvement is accomplished only by training well and consistently.

On the downside, mountain bikes are ill suited to longer-distance riding and touring. As a result, many people are dusting off their old 10-speeds or purchasing good-quality road bikes.

Then again, you don't even have to go outside to go cycling. Some people actually prefer stationary bikes. Local gyms usually have a string of them; they are ridden by people who prefer reading magazines to dodging tree trunks in the forest. Stationary bikes can be ridden through all kinds of weather and can even be pushed in front of the TV set for those who want to combine fitness with entertainment.

Cross-country skiing

Skiing can be hard work, whether you're riding the lift to get to the slopes or going cross-country. Cross-country skiing's big advantage over its downhill cousin is its low cost: not only is there no outlay for lift tickets, but the equipment you need can be less expensive, too.

Cross-country skiing provides an excellent cardio workout and, as with cycling, there's very little of the jarring and pounding associated with running. Cross-country skiing tests just about every muscle in your body—including the large muscles of your arms, shoulders, torso, back and legs—which makes it the ideal all-round workout.

If you're lucky enough to live in an area where cross-country skiing is an option, you will probably discover numerous skiers as dedicated and loyal to this sport as runners are to theirs.

Aerobics (exercise to music)

Some men turn up their noses at aerobics to music because it has been deemed a feminine activity. It's their loss. Women do make up the biggest chunk of participants, but these women can be very, very fit. They have discovered that pounding music, a group atmosphere and having someone calling out moves is highly motivating, and that the fitness results can be astounding. If you decide aerobics is for you, consider three factors to avoid injury. First, choose a low-impact class. The majority of aerobics classes are modeled along the step-program format, which is low-impact, so you shouldn't have much trouble finding one that's suitable. Second, make sure you won't be exercising on concrete. Third, check that the class is led by a qualified instructor.

In-line skating

In-line skating gets more popular every year as skates go down in price and up in quality. In-line skating can be done just about anywhere there are paved surfaces, which is a mixed blessing because blades and cars don't mix very well—all that sideways motion by skaters makes them a hazard, both for the cars and themselves. Provided you can find a safe place to do it, in-line skating will give you an excellent cardio workout and help build your muscular strength and endurance.

In-line skating is particularly good for strengthening the vastus medialis, the inside muscle of the quadriceps at the front of the upper leg, which is chronically underdeveloped in runners. Running develops the vastus lateralis, the outside muscle of the quad, so developing the vastus medialis will help you create balanced strength, to better support the knee joint.

In-line skating is low-impact—unless, of course, you fall. It's best to take some lessons and essential to wear the proper gear: wrist guards and a helmet are mandatory (a good bike helmet will do), and knee pads and elbow pads are strongly recommended. And stay off busy streets, because all the padding in the world won't help you if you collide with a car.

Climbing

Climbing is another sport on the grow, for sound reasons: it provides not only a good workout but numerous life lessons as well. Most people have a healthy fear of heights; assuming you're among them, when the going gets steep, you normally want to stay away from the cliff edge. In a climbing environment with ropes and harnesses, even though the safety system is extremely reliable, your mind responds to the danger. You're off the ground, if you fall you die, and it says, "Get back!" Of course, because you're there to climb, you don't "get back"; you keep going and you learn to work with fear. As self-help books have been telling us for years, groundless fear is what prevents many people from realizing their true potential, so sometimes pushing back the mental boundaries can be just as useful as pushing back the physical ones.

As a workout, climbing is good for developing muscular power and endurance as well, because you can be on the wall for a long time working out the moves. Climbers tend to have strong forearms, triceps, abdominals, back muscles, quadriceps, hamstrings, calves, ankles and feet.

(A lot of that finger strength, by the way, comes from the forearm.) As with in-line skating, climbing is low-impact unless you fall. Although it's extremely rare for anyone to fall if the safety system is used correctly, climbing is still an inherently dangerous sport, so proper training is highly recommended. Most larger urban centers have indoor climbing facilities and most of these offer training programs.

Strength Training

Some runners don't strength train because, they say, they lose speed if they bulk up. This is a myth. Strength training is vital to the development of speed. Although you can become a capable runner without working with weights, increasing muscle tone by strength training will help— and make running more enjoyable as well.

The main reason to strength train is that it can assist you in developing your muscles in a more balanced way, which reduces the risk of injury. Injuries tend to occur when muscle strength is insufficient to support weaknesses, whether those are naturally occurring or have been introduced by previous injuries. For example, if you sprained your ankle or twisted your knee when you were a teenager, there may be lingering scar tissue around these joints. By increasing the strength around these old injuries you can give the joints the support they need to keep the injuries from flaring up again.

Muscle groups are generally arranged in an opposing fashion and while one contracts, the other relaxes (in support of the movement). As a runner, you will be most concerned about the opposing groups that include the

Checklist for strength training

- Get advice from a fitness professional
- Before each workout, warm up properly
- Begin by working with lighter weights
- Start out with one or two sets of 10–15 repetitions for each exercise
- Train 2–3 times per week
- Over time, gradually increase the weight or resistance

quadriceps and hamstring combination, the abdominal and lower back muscles, and the calf and anterior shin muscles (those at the front of your leg below your knee) Some sample exercises are provided on pages 156–60.

As well as helping to prevent injury, strength training can help prevent the decrease in muscle mass that occurs with age (usually the result of reduced activity and the aging process itself), thereby lessening your susceptibility to osteoporosis and other diseases. Studies have shown that even the elderly can increase their muscle mass and enhance their bone density through strength training.

Finally, increasing your strength has a psychological benefit, too: feeling strong feels good. Although weight training and variations thereof that lead to increased muscle strength can be tedious in the beginning, in time it can be very satisfying to flex a muscle and feel the strength in it.

Darren

Darren loved running and wanted to be strong, but hated lifting weights. "It's so boring," says the 34-year-old police officer. "But you have to be strong, because in this job you never know when you're going to have to do a little wrestling." Then one day he met a recruit with a vise-like grip who looked like he had been born in a gym. "I asked how many days a week he lifted and he said 'none.' I asked him what kinds of drugs he was using and he laughed at me," Darren recalls. Darren's new friend turned out to be a rock climber—the reason he was so strong was that he had started climbing at the age of 10. "The guy was solid steel and he never lifted weights. At least, not exactly. When he was climbing, he was lifting his own body weight all the time."

Darren started going to the local climbing gym, and after a course of instruction he bought his own harness and climbing shoes. "I'm stronger now than I've ever been in my life, and I never get bored—there's always something new to climb and you're too busy figuring out the moves."

Cautions

Before embarking on any strength-training program, you should get instruction on technique from a qualified trainer, especially if you're using free weights.

Even if you do most of your strengthening with gym equipment, it's best not to rely on machines alone, as they tend to allow very specific, often limited ranges of motion. (The strength you develop will be focused in the ranges that you are working.) Free weights can provide more variety and a greater range of motion. Strength training exercises have even been developed for working on large "physio" balls (see suggested strength training exercises for runners on pages 158–60).

Start with light weights and do a larger number of repetitions. As you become more skilled and/or wish to gain greater strength, you can decrease the number of repetitions and increase the weight.

No matter what your age or fitness level, give yourself 48 hours between strength-training sessions. Strength training can be hard on muscles and it is very likely that your muscles will feel sore for a day or two after your session. Part of this soreness is due to minute tears in the muscle caused by the exercise. Given sufficient time, the muscles will knit back together to be stronger and more efficient. But if you don't give your body enough time to recover, you can do yourself more harm than good. This is especially true when you begin; as you get stronger, you will find you can push your limits further.

Although you may be developing muscles in order to run, this does not mean you should develop only the

✓ Women are catching up. A study at the University of California showed that elite women runners have been improving twice as fast as elite men runners over the last three decades—46 feet (14 meters) per minute per decade versus 23 feet (7 meters) per minute for men.

How do I avoid injuries?

- You don't need to exercise every day to maintain or improve your fitness level—one hour 3–4 times a week is adequate
- Get enough rest
- Pay attention to your body; if you have an ache or a pain, try cross training until you are injury free
- It's not true that two to three days away from your walk/run program is a bad thing—cross training will keep you fit
- When you resume your walk/run routine, start back where you left off

—Olympian Lynn Kanuka

muscles in your lower body. Upper body strength is necessary for good running posture. For example, if your erector spine muscles (in your back) are weak, you will find it more difficult to stand up straight when you run and will tend to lean forward. This in turn will decrease your stride and your endurance.

One last warning: At some gyms, people hang around selling various drugs and supplements they promise will help you get stronger faster. Even if that's true, it's certainly a case of short-term gain for long-term pain. Drugs can do irreparable harm to your body.

Hill running

Why run hills? Maybe you live in a city such as San Francisco or Vancouver where it is hard to avoid them. Maybe you want to improve your running fitness so that you can run longer and faster. Whatever your reasons, running hills can be both rewarding and tough.

Running hills works your body both aerobically and anaerobically during the same session. As with lifting weights, this type of running is resistance training. As you build your muscle strength and endurance, your legs will get stronger and you won't tire as quickly. Over time, knowing that you can run up—and down—hills will bolster your confidence and give you a whole lot of new places to train.

When you first start to run hills:

1. Pick one small, short hill to start.
2. Start slowly. Pay attention to what muscles your body is using as you climb.
3. Run a short distance to start; 1–2 minutes is enough.

If the hill is longer than this, take a walking break and then try to continue to the top.

4. When you get to the top, jog or walk slowly back down the hill.

5. Repeat the slow run up and walk down 2–4 times to start.

6. Listen to your body; if your muscles are straining or you're having trouble breathing, slow down.

7. Once you can comfortably run up and down your chosen hill, you can challenge yourself by increasing the length or grade of the hill, the number of intervals (the number of times you run fast up and slowly down) or the speed of your run. Be careful not to do too much too far too fast. Also remember that running downhill places a lot of stress on your joints, so take it easy!

Stretching

Chapter 3 discussed the need for warm-up and cool-down stretches, and sample exercises are provided on pages 156–57. A few points are worth mentioning again. Stretching can make you a better runner by increasing your flexibility. Don't forget to warm up gently first with some walking or on-the-spot jogging. Should you feel particularly tight, knead your muscles between your fingers to get the blood flowing. (If you have a running partner, you can massage each other's muscles when necessary.) Ease into your stretching routine and stick to light stretching before your workout, saving your deeper and longer stretching program for after your run. Stretch before and after every run.

Running Technique

Technique isn't likely to hold you back when you first start running, but the faster and farther you go, the more likely it is to affect your performance. Good running technique can often be judged both visually and from within; if the running feels smooth and efficient, it probably is.

A great way to get feedback on your running technique is to join a running group. Such groups usually include runners of varying abilities, some of whom should be able to help you improve your performance.

This section describes a few basic components of good form for both running and walking. It's not necessary to memorize the list. Instead, as you read it through, think about your own running style, one component at a time. Keep in mind that the most important thing you can do to improve your running technique is relax.

Positioning

Feet

Your feet should point straight ahead and be positioned parallel to one another. When each foot strikes the ground, it should be directly underneath your hip.

Thighs

When your left foot strikes the ground, your left thigh should accelerate backward while your right thigh moves forward (and vice versa).

Hips

Your hips should be flexible, allowing for a longer, more efficient stride.

Torso

Your torso should be erect, with your pelvis tucked in (neutral position). Visualize running tall.

Shoulders and arms

Your arms should swing naturally, starting at the shoulder joint. Walkers should keep their arms slightly bent at the elbow, their wrists relaxed, whereas runners should bend their arms at the elbow and keep their hands cupped. Runners should also focus on keeping their shoulders square and driving their arms backward, which will create a rebound effect, sending the arms forward.

Common problems

Beginning runners especially will want to watch for these common problems.

Overstriding

Overstriding occurs when, during an effort to increase stride length, the knee locks as you reach with the lead foot. The lead foot then lands in front of your center of gravity, causing jarring and braking. In this position, the knee is less able to absorb shock and sooner or later pain results. To eliminate overstriding, be sure that with each stride your foot strikes the ground under your hip and with the knee slightly flexed.

Upper-body twisting

Running and walking are generally linear activities. If you allow your upper body to twist too much, energy that should be used to direct the body forward is expended in wasted rotational motion. What's more, if your upper

The runner's stance

Body Upright

Head Chin up, eyes looking straight ahead

Arms Swinging naturally, elbow bent to form a right angle

Feet Push-off with toes; land mid-foot

To avoid tension

When training hard, tension in the upper body is common.

- Try pressing your thumb and one of your fingers together to remove stress in the shoulders and back. You have to try it to believe that it works

—*Olympian Lynn Kanuka*

body twists, your arms and feet tend to follow and cross the midline. Not only is this style of running or walking inefficient, it increases your chances of being injured. Concentrate on moving your arms through 90 degrees while keeping your body square.

High hands, hunched shoulders

When fatigue sets in, your hands will tend to rise and your shoulders to hunch. This leads to increased tension in the muscles of the upper body and wastes energy. Your shoulders and hands need to stay relaxed and loose. To ensure that they do, concentrate on your posture: head up and eyes focused ahead; shoulders square, pulled back and down; chest lifted and abdominal muscles contracted (pressed towards your spine); pelvis in a neutral position.

Shuffling

Runners who shuffle typically fail to lift their knees high enough and may swing their arms and hips too much to compensate. Developing adequate hip-to-knee flexibility and strength can help solve this problem; the hip flexor stretch on page 157 should help.

7
Fueling the Body

A CAR WON'T GO WITHOUT THE PROPER FUEL IN ITS TANK, nor will your body. No matter how much or how little you exercise, whether you are trying to lose weight or put it on, you have to feed your body healthfully to make it work well.

This is true for everyone, but especially for runners. Exercise can be hard on the body—even the exercise in the 13-week walk/run program, which is designed to minimize that hardship. Ignore your body's need for proper fuel and you will put yourself at increased risk for fatigue, injury and disease. Pay attention to the care and feeding of your body and it will respond to the demands of exercise by getting stronger. Not only will your training sessions be more productive, but you will feel better during them. Your recovery times will be shorter, too.

Patricia Chuey, a registered dietitian/nutritionist and the author of *The 101 Most Asked Nutrition Questions,* is amazed by how many people ignore their basic nutritional needs. "People make so many mistakes when it comes to nutrition. It seems we've been socialized into bad habits. If people take a break in their day, they usually sit around and have a coffee! Or they decide to unwind

Don't deny yourself the things you love to eat—just be moderate.

after work by drinking alcohol and eating salty peanuts or pretzels."

Sue Crawford, a registered dietitian with a Ph.D. in kinesiology, understands that it's sometimes hard for people to eat nutritiously in today's busy world. "It takes a lot of thought to get into the habit of eating properly," she says. "Inappropriate foods are always the ones being pushed." But there are good reasons to resist the stream of junk food coming at you. If you don't provide your body with the nutrients it requires, the consequences can range from being tired or getting sick (colds and the flu) more often to getting heart disease or cancer.

Healthy Eating

The three keys to healthy eating are balance, variety and moderation. A fourth key can be added in these times of highly processed "fast foods," namely that food be as close to natural as possible.

Balance is about eating from all the main food categories, including fruits, vegetables, grains, legumes (beans), meat and dairy products—with exceptions, of course, for those who choose to follow a form of vegetarian diet. Remember that no one food group can provide you with all the nutrients you need. A slab of steak with a few peas on the side is not a balanced meal, nor is pasta every day for a month supplemented by the occasional trip to the salad bar.

Variety means choosing a selection of foods from each main group every day to ensure a healthy diet. No single food, no matter how nutritious, should dominate your diet or even your intake from one group. Oranges, for example, provide a lot of vitamin C, but eating oranges to the exclusion of other wonderful fruits such as apples, pears, melons and bananas—each of which has different nutritional strengths—will not result in optimum health.

Moderation ensures that you eat neither too much nor too little. Dietitians suggest at least five servings of grain products and five servings of fruits and vegetables every day. If milk products are part of your diet, nutritionists suggest at least two servings of them per day (three to four for adolescents and pregnant or nursing women). As well, each person should eat two servings of meat or alternative sources of protein (e.g., tofu, baked beans) per day. So, what's a serving? The following would all constitute an average "serving": a slice of bread, a bowl of cereal, a banana, a potato, 1–1$^1/_2$ cups (200–300 mL) of cooked beans, two eggs or 3 ounces (85 grams) of meat— which is about the same size as a pack of playing cards. Vegetarians who eat eggs and dairy products (also known as ovo-lacto vegetarians) and those who eat only dairy products (called lacto-vegetarians) must rely on fruits, vegetables, grains, beans, nuts and seeds for the nutrients provided by the meat group. Vegans, who eat neither eggs nor dairy products, rely on those same groups for the nutrients provided by the dairy group as well as the meat group. For vegans, fortified soy products are especially rich, useful sources of nutrients.

"Natural foods" might conjure up images of health-food stores, but the phrase really just means foods that either are not processed or are processed as little as possible. Such foods tend to be better for you because they generally contain more nutrients and fewer additives (such as fats) than foods that have been more heavily processed. For example, potatoes are better for you than potato chips, bread made from whole wheat flour is better than bread made from white flour and apples are better than apple juice. This is not to say that junk food must never again pass your lips, just that it should play a minor role in your diet.

Low-Carbohydrate Diets

Never before have North Americans been this unhealthy and overweight. Today's fast-food culture has changed not only how we eat but how much. It's not surprising that low-carbohydrate diets that promise quick and easy solutions to their weight-loss woes have millions of North Americans eating little more than steak, bacon and cheese.

High-protein, low-carbohydrate diets first became popular in the 1970s and then again in the early part of the 21st century. These diets, which advocate eating large amounts of protein while discouraging the intake of carbohydrates, present people of all shapes and sizes with novel options to weight loss that are easy to follow. From the sedentary father who wants to lose 20 pounds (9 kilograms) and gain energy to the athlete looking for a leaner physique, a low-carb diet does, at least initially, produce weight loss.

The "science" behind low-carb diets

One of the less understood issues about low-carbohydrate diets is how they initially promote rapid weight loss. According to sport dietitian Dallas Parsons, "The body mainly stores carbohydrate in the liver and muscle tissue.

For every gram of stored carbohydrate (glycogen), the body may store up to .1 ounces (3 grams) of water. When people stop eating carbohydrate-containing foods, they become glycogen depleted, which also results in body fluid losses." The result of this diuretic effect is rapid weight loss, but not of body fat. As well, according to Dallas, these diets induce a condition called ketosis, which suppresses appetite and leads to reduced caloric intake.

When carbohydrates are reintroduced into the diet, the body stores them together with water. Subsequently, dieters see an immediate weight gain and perceive this to be a gain in fat tissue, which is not the case—it is mostly water. This is how carbohydrates get a bad rap. It is critically important to understand that the body needs a constant supply of carbohydrates for everyday functioning of the brain and muscles as well as for purposeful exercise, such as running. The few extra pounds that result with the reintroduction of fruits, vegetables and whole grains supply a healthy dose of fuel and fluid that is vital to sport performance.

What is not widely known about low-carb diets

- A diet that's low in carbohydrates and high in protein often produces immediate weight loss, but rarely results in a permanent reduction in weight.
- A large percentage of low-carb dieters find this diet regime too restrictive to adopt for a lifetime.
- Protein and high-fat foods are rich and satiating, but dieters quickly become bored and begin to crave carbohydrates.

The downside of low-carb diets

- A high intake of low-fiber high-fat foods can cause constipation

- A limited intake of fruits, vegetables and whole grains leaves most people feeling sluggish, light-headed, moody and unable to concentrate

- Active people experience decreased energy and a decreased desire to exercise—a breeding ground for poor athletic performance

- Vegetarians typically have difficulty following a low-carb diet because their food choices become extremely limited.

- A low-carb diet is high in saturated fat. Many studies show that diets high in saturated fat pose significant health risks.

- Low-carbohydrate diets are short-term solutions to weight loss or weight control because they are not practical. Restricting the intake of carbohydrates eliminates many mixed meals (such as casseroles), limits easy-to-prepare meal options (such as sandwiches) and complicates eating away from home.

Running in a low-carb haze

Fats and protein are not "clean" sources of fuel; when exercisers are forced to use them as fuel sources they don't feel good. Studies show that the affects of a low-carb diet on athletes is far reaching. It has been well-proven that these individuals fatigue earlier, have less coordination and experience more irritability than athletes eating a balanced diet. So what do dietitians suggest *is* a good diet for regular exercisers? Sport dietitian Patricia Chuey recommends "high-carb foods with a high glycemic index, including bananas, bagels, energy bars and sport drinks. While shunned by low-carb dieters, these foods are easily converted into energy and sugar and are well-loved by athletes because they promote faster recovery." As Chuey notes, carbs are still the main source of energy for active people. Without carbs, runners and other athletes report low energy and reduced ability to perform.

The Ideal Runner's Diet

Runners typically train on a daily basis. Subsequently, their food intake has a significant impact on their performance, recovery and overall health. No matter how many hours they put in on a weekly basis, their bodies require that they choose the right amount and types of foods at the appropriate times of day. To attain the maximum benefit from their running programs, runners must satisfy the nutritional demands placed upon their bodies by running.

Sport dietitian Dallas Parsons stresses that "the ideal runner's diet consists of large amounts of carbohydrate-rich foods, including whole-grain breads and high-fiber cereals as well as red, orange and deep-green fruits and vegetables. These foods provide runners with the fuel they need to complete their daily workouts, plus vitamins, minerals and anti-oxidants to aid in recovery."

Parsons also urges runners to regularly include high-quality protein foods such as meat, poultry, fish and tofu in their diets. These foods supply amino acids, iron and zinc for muscle repair, oxygen delivery and proper immune function. As female distance runners may be at a greater risk than their male counterparts of becoming iron deficient, it is particularly important that they incorporate protein into their diet on a daily basis. Calcium, which is involved in muscle contractions, nerve transmissions, carbohydrate metabolism and bone maintenance, is another important ingredient in the runner's diet. Besides dairy products, fortified soy products, juice beverages and dark-green leafy vegetables can supply this vital nutrient.

Losing weight

People think that if they do a lot of running, they'll suddenly lose weight. But I've seen 5- and 10-k runners lose more weight than half-marathon runners, because they did fast interval training—versus the long, slow miles of marathon training.

Losing weight requires burning calories *and* speeding up your metabolism, which happens when you increase your heart rate by running *faster.*
—*Olympian Lynn Kanuka*

In addition to food, fluid is an essential component of running performance and overall health. The perfect runner's diet includes adequate fluid intake—before, during and after exercise—to ensure that the body's internal functions, such as nutrient delivery, temperature regulation and removal of wastes, are operating at optimal levels. This is particularly important when running in warm environments.

RUNNER PROFILE

Sarah

Sarah had been running for a few years and had always maintained a healthy weight. However, after two weeks at her folks' place over the Christmas holidays, the 27-year-old teacher found that her pants were suddenly much tighter. While Sarah was happy that she had enjoyed her visit home, including her mother's baking and her father's eggnog, she definitely wasn't happy about the 10 extra pounds (4.5 kilograms) she was now carrying.

After listening to numerous colleagues discussing their quick results and reading similar stories in the tabloids at her grocery store checkout, Sarah decided to give a low-carb diet a try. She was amazed: after a couple of weeks she had already lost several pounds and was feeling more comfortable in her clothing, and was quickly approaching her 10-pound weight-loss goal. The only glitch was her lack of energy.

Prior to going on the diet, Sarah had had no trouble finding the motivation to run three times a week and walk her dog after work. Now, she was lucky if she ran once a week. Her energy was drastically reduced and her running partners had started to ask if she was sick or under the weather. When she did walk or run, she often felt light-headed and moody. Another thing Sarah noticed was how she was fantasizing about carbohydrates: bagels, pasta and cookies!

After two weeks on her low-carb diet, Sarah had lost eight pounds and her sugar cravings seemed to have decreased. As she reintroduced carbs into her diet, she gained a few pounds but her energy was almost back to normal. She is happier now and feeling more like her old self. She likes the fact that her pants fit better, but she didn't like how the diet altered her moods and energy. After talking to a dietician, she now tries to limit refined and processed foods in favor of more nutritious alternatives such as beans, fruits and whole-grain breads. And while she hasn't achieved her original weight-loss goal, she feels healthier and has more energy for her active lifestyle.

Planning Makes Perfect

Eating right takes planning. Although you don't have to become an expert on the nutritional values of food, you will find it easier to stay healthy if you understand the basic ingredients of a healthy diet and keep those ingredients in mind when you shop. If you're used to living on fast foods or depending on processed foods, it may take you a while to adjust.

Pre-packaged foods and instant meals are often designed to capitalize on food fads; they also usually sell taste and appearance rather than good nutrition. These convenience food products can be part of a nutritious and quickly prepared meal, but you will want to read labels carefully and avoid foods with ingredients that research has shown may be harmful. For instance, hydrogenated oils can contribute to heart disease, and preservatives called nitrites have been associated with some forms of cancer, so you'll want to avoid these.

Put simply, you eat food so that your body can extract from it the nutrients, including minerals and vitamins, it needs to survive. No matter what kind of diet you live on, whether you eat flesh foods or not, whether you knock back milk like a teenager or avoid it altogether, your cells are looking for some basic elements to do their job. The body uses carbohydrates, protein and fat from food to create fuel for itself.

Carbohydrates

Carbohydrates are a vital source of energy that fuels both your brain and your muscles. They are abundant in any food in the grain group, such as rice, pasta, bread and

"Balance" and moderation are key. Enjoy a *piece* of cake—*not* the whole cake.
—*Olympian Lynn Kanuka*

Bananas are a runner's best friend. They are—

- easily digested
- an instant, natural energy source
- a no-performance-consequence fruit—unlike apples (too much fiber) or oranges (too acidic)

—*Olympian Lynn Kanuka*

crackers; fruits and their juices; vegetables, and, to a lesser extent, dairy products and legumes.

Carbohydrates are important, especially for athletes, because they can be rapidly converted into glucose—which is the scientific name for the simple sugar that circulates in your bloodstream. Unlike proteins and fat, carbohydrates break down quickly; some can serve almost immediately as fuel for your brain and muscles. As well, extra glucose can be stored in your muscles and liver as glycogen, which is the main source of fuel for muscle movement. Human beings have a low capacity for storing glycogen, which is why you need to replace it constantly.

Perhaps you are wondering if it wouldn't be best to introduce sugar directly into your system, instead of eating forms of carbohydrates that have to be broken down first. There are good reasons why you shouldn't. The main one is that sugar is a nutritionally deficient fuel, supplying calories but none of the other things you need at the same time, such as vitamins, minerals, antioxidants and protein.

On balance, about 55 to 60 per cent of your daily caloric intake should come from carbohydrate sources. The daily requirement for carbohydrate consumption is 0.14 to 0.18 ounces (4 to 5 grams) per 2.2 pounds (1 kilogram) of body weight. Having heard that carbohydrates are a power food, some athletes load up on them to the wrongful exclusion of other important nutrients. It is not uncommon for athletes to get 80 per cent of their calories from carbohydrates. But going this route can deprive the body of other important nutrients.

Another health concern is that the majority of North Americans get most of their carbohydrate calories from foods like pasta and bread, and not enough from fruits and vegetables. Ironically, many vegetarians fall into this camp. "Grain-atarian might be a better word to describe a lot of vegetarians I see," Chuey says. "They tend to be eating all kinds of rice and pasta and not enough fruits and vegetables. The thing with regular pasta is that it's really just white bread in the shape of noodles, unless it's whole-grain pasta. I'm always trying to get vegetarians to eat more vegetables. Eating different grains is a good idea too." Although pasta seems to be the carb of choice for athletes, it's a good idea to add variety to your diet by including some of the other grains—for example, brown rice, barley and oatmeal. At the very least, use whole-grain pasta whenever possible.

Protein is essential not just for children but for adults as well. It helps build and repair muscles, red blood cells, hair and other tissues. It also helps in synthesizing hormones.

Protein

Protein is another essential ingredient in a balanced diet; it should make up 15 to 20 per cent of your caloric intake. Experts recommend a daily intake of 0.03 ounces (0.8 grams) of protein per 2.2 pounds (1 kilogram) of body weight. For a highly active person this can increase to as much as 0.05 ounces (1.5 grams) per 2.2 pounds per day.

Protein is a requirement for the normal growth and maintenance of every cell in the body. Chuey says people easily recognize why children, who are growing, need protein, but have more difficulty understanding its importance to adults. In fact, the muscle fibers and cells in each person's body are constantly breaking down, especially if one is subjected to stress, whether emotional or physical. The body needs to recover and rebuild, and in order to do that it needs protein. By and large, however, an athlete

✔ Trying to lose weight by going on a starvation diet and running won't work. Strenuous exercise paired with inadequate calories will cause the body to conserve its stored fat.

does not need more protein per unit of body weight than an inactive person does, and the average North American already eats more than enough protein. Excess protein—whether eaten as food or acquired through supplements—can be stored as fat and can, under some circumstances, cause dehydration.

Protein is found in greatest proportion in meat (including fish and seafood), eggs, dairy products (including milk, cheese and yogurt) and all kinds of legumes (including lentils and beans). Chuey and other dietitians, not to mention vegetarians, rate soy products such as tofu and soy milk as being among the healthiest sources of protein. Many people avoid beans, complaining of gas, but that's circular logic because the body can't produce the enzymes needed to digest them unless it's regularly exposed to beans. If you eat more beans, you will eventually digest them more easily and your gas problems should decrease.

Fat

Although too much fat is bad for you, no fat at all is even worse. Of course, it's important to distinguish between healthy and unhealthy fats.

The healthiest fat sources include omega-3 fatty acids, which are critical nutrients; your body uses them to produce certain chemicals it needs to function. Omega-3 fatty acids are found in fish, shellfish, soy products, walnuts, canola oil, flax oil, wheat germ and green leafy vegetables. Monounsaturated fats are also healthy, because they help lower the levels of harmful cholesterol (LDL) and raise the level of the good kind (HDL). Monounsaturated fats are found in olives, olive oil, almonds, canola oil, peanuts and avocados. Much of the fat you eat should come from these types of sources.

Polyunsaturated fat, which is found in safflower, corn and sunflower oils, is also healthy, but less so than the omega-3 or monounsaturated types.

Saturated fats, the kind found in red meat, whole-milk products (including many cheeses) and such plant sources as cocoa butter, coconut oil and palm oil, are best consumed in small amounts. Finally, it's a good idea to minimize your intake of fats that contain trans-fatty acids. These forms are rare in nature but common in highly processed products made from hydrogenated plant oils. Manufactured foods high in trans-fatty acids include some margarines and many fast foods, snack foods, commercially baked goods (cookies, muffins, cakes) and baking mixes.

If you're trying to lose weight, eliminating fat from your diet is exactly the wrong way to go. You need fat to burn as fuel. If you eliminate fat from your diet, your body interprets it as a starvation message and instead of throwing its fat reserves into the fire, it holds on to them for as long as it can. Avoiding all fats is not a long-term solution to weight loss.

Vitamins and Minerals

Vitamins

Vitamins are metabolic catalysts that regulate chemical reactions within the body. If you have a balanced diet and take in the right amount of calories, your need for vitamin supplements will probably be very low. If not, it's alright to supplement your diet with a balanced multivitamin and multimineral, but don't delude yourself into thinking that popping pills is in any way a substitute for good nutrition: it's for good reason they're called supplements, not replacements.

Vitamin A is found in milk products and vegetables; vitamin C in some fruits and vegetables; B vitamins (including thiamin, riboflavin, niacin, folacin, B_6 and B_{12}) in meat, whole grains, yeast, green leafy vegetables and soybeans; vitamin D in egg yolks, fish liver oils, fortified milk and soy milk products; vitamin E in wheat germ and whole-grain cereals, and vitamin K in many vegetables, especially green leafy ones.

The sources of B vitamins vary quite widely, so deserve extra attention. Vitamin B_1 (thiamin) is found in breads, cereals, nuts, pork and ham; vitamin B_2 (riboflavin) in

RUNNER PROFILE

Gayleen

Long before Gayleen started running, she knew the ins and outs of good nutrition. She'd been brought up to believe in the benefits of fruits and vegetables, and she tended to avoid the bad fats by default; she just didn't like greasy foods. "I felt I was way ahead of the game and didn't really need to pay too much attention to changing my eating habits when I started running," says the 49-year-old professor.

The issue that emerged for her wasn't so much what to eat and how much, but when. "Everybody seemed to have a different theory. I like to run when I get home from work in the afternoon. Some people told me I should eat something before I run and some said after." Sara tried snacking before her afternoon run but she always felt sluggish.

"Eventually I figured out what was right for me," she says. "Now I avoid eating before my run—except for lunch, of course. Instead, I like to eat right after running. Sometimes my partner and I even pick a route so we can finish up someplace where we can eat."

milk, cheese, liver, breads and cereals, and vitamin B_3 (niacin) in meat, fish, poultry, breads, cereals and nuts.

The member of the B-vitamin family called folacin or folic acid, which is found in green leafy vegetables, wheat germ, beans and citrus products, is essential to cell division in the body. Because the need for folic acid therefore rises dramatically during pregnancy, all women of child-bearing age should take a folic acid supplement; doing so has been proven to reduce the risk of some types of birth defects. The recommended supplemental dose for healthy adults is about 400 micrograms, doubling to 800 micrograms for pregnant women.

Vitamin B_{12} is vital not only to maintain the health of your nervous system but to form blood cells. B_{12} occurs naturally in all animal products (meat and dairy), but not in any plant products, which is why it is the most problematic nutrient for vegans. However, a number of food products are fortified with B_{12}, including fortified soy milk and breakfast cereals; simulated egg, meat and dairy products; some meal replacement formulas, and nutritional yeast grown on a vitamin B_{12}-enriched medium. Vitamin B_{12} supplements are also available.

Minerals

Like vitamins, minerals are vital to your body's processes. Some of the more important ones are calcium, magnesium, phosphorous, sodium, potassium and zinc.

Calcium is an important nutrient for bone health and strength—from childhood growth, throughout an athletic career and into old age. Women, especially, should be sure

Although there may seem to be a lot of rules associated with healthy eating, the rules still leave room for personal choices. Provided you eat a balanced diet and get the vitamins, minerals and other nutrients your body needs, you can establish eating patterns that best complement your life and running schedule.

they take in enough calcium as they need to establish good bone density before the losses associated with menopause occur. Both sexes start losing bone mass after age 35, but because women have smaller bones to begin with, they're much more likely to suffer fractures. Complicating the issue for women is that at menopause estrogen levels decline, further speeding the loss of bone mass. Current recommendations call for about 1,000 milligrams of calcium per day for males and adult females through to age 50, and 1,500 milligrams per day for females over 50. It's also important to keep in mind that calcium alone does not make strong bones. It takes weight-bearing exercise, and, for women, normal estrogen levels, to build and keep them.

Like other nutrients, calcium is best obtained from food sources. Milk, for example, contains not only calcium but also a protein that encourages stomach acid secretions that aid calcium absorption. The lactose (a form of sugar) in milk also helps with absorption, as do vitamins C and D (the latter comes to us from sunshine, and is usually added to milk). Other good sources of calcium include canned salmon, firm tofu (made with calcium), fortified soy milk, dark leafy vegetables, sesame seeds and figs. It's a good idea to aim for at least three to four servings of calcium and/or milk products per day. For a list of foods that are a good source of calcium, see page 113.

Note: If you're not getting enough calcium in your diet, you may want to consider taking a calcium supplement. Calcium citrate and calcium malate are generally the most easily absorbed; it's best to take these supplements with food. Keep in mind that no matter how you get your calcium, if you take in alcohol, caffeine, salt or too much protein, you'll lose more of the calcium you take in.

Potassium, another important mineral, is found in bananas, most fruits, and potatoes. Potassium helps your body to transmit nerve impulses and helps your muscles to contract.

Food	Portion size	Milligrams of calcium
Dairy products		
Milk (whole, 2%, 1% or skim)	1 cup (250 mL)	300
Yogurt, low fat, plain	³/₄ cup (175 mL)	300
Cheese, Swiss	1 oz (30 g)	240
Cheese, brick or cheddar	1 oz (30 g)	205
Processed cheese slices, cheddar	1 oz (30 g)	170
Milk, evaporated whole	¹/₄ cup (60 mL)	165
Cottage cheese	1 cup (250 mL)	140
Ice cream	¹/₂ cup (125 mL)	85
Fish		
Sardines, canned, with bones	8 medium	370
Salmon, canned, with bones	3 oz (85 g)	190
Plant Foods		
Calcium-fortified soy or rice beverage	1 cup (250 mL)	300*
Blackstrap molasses	1 tbsp (15 mL)	170
Bok choy, cooked	1 cup (250 mL)	150
Tofu, firm (made with calcium)	¹/₄ cup (60 mL)	125*
Whole sesame seeds	1 tbsp (15 mL)	90
Tahini (sesame seed butter)	1 tbsp (15 mL)	63
Orange	1 medium	55
Almond butter	1 tbsp (15 mL)	43
Pinto beans or chick peas	¹/₂ cup (125 mL)	40
Broccoli, cooked	¹/₂ cup (125 mL)	35
Tomatoes, canned	¹/₂ cup (125 mL)	35

*Varies with manufacturer. Be sure to check labels.
Source: Dial-A-Dietitian Nutrition Information Society of B.C.

Iron is an essential component of hemoglobin, the blood protein that transports oxygen from the lungs to the working muscles. Iron deficiencies can lead to premature fatigue. Athletes who ignore their iron intake are at risk for iron-deficiency anemia, as are women in general, as they lose considerable amounts of iron through menstruation. It is unwise to self-diagnose fatigue as iron deficiency and then self-prescribe supplements, because although iron is vital to your body, too much is toxic and can interfere with the absorption of such minerals as zinc and copper. Consult your physician before taking any type of iron supplement.

Ideally, you should get your iron from food. Good sources include meat, liver, dried peas and beans, asparagus, leafy dark-green vegetables, dried fruits, whole grains, prune juice and iron-enriched breads and cereals (check labels to see that they say "iron enriched"; if they don't say the products are enriched, they aren't). Iron is hard to absorb, so even when it's in the food you eat, your body

Food	Portion size	Milligrams of iron
Plant Sources		
Bran cereal with raisins	1 cup (250 mL)	9
Tofu (varies by brand; check labels)	½ cup (125 mL)	7
Potato (with skin)	1 medium	2.75
Pinto beans or chickpeas	½ cup (125 mL)	2.25
Parsley	½ cup (125 mL)	2
Raisins	½ cup (125 mL)	2
Dried apricots	10 (whole)	2
Broccoli	1 cup (250 mL)	1.3
Bread, enriched	1 slice	1

can't necessarily use it. This is particularly true of iron from plant sources. You can dramatically increase your iron absorption, however, by eating iron-rich foods with foods rich in vitamin C; consider having a big glass of orange juice with your morning cereal or toast. Other good sources of vitamin C include broccoli, potatoes, strawberries, tomatoes, cabbage and leafy dark-green vegetables. In addition, you can increase your iron intake simply by cooking with iron pots and pans, which is how people from other cultures who do not eat meat, or who eat very little of it, get much of their iron.

Absorption of iron can also be blocked by certain foods. Fiber, tannins in tea and coffee, and other chemicals naturally occurring in food can all inhibit iron absorption.

The U.S. recommended daily allowance for iron is 10 milligrams per day for men and 15 for women. Health Canada recommends 8 mg for men and 14 for women. Below and on page 114 are lists of some dietary sources of iron.

Food	Portion size	Milligrams of iron
Animal Sources		
Clams	10 (medium-size)	10
Beef liver	3 oz (85 g)	7
Oysters	6	6
Beef	3 oz (85 g)	4
Turkey (dark meat)	4 oz (110 g)	2.6
Turkey (light meat)	4 oz (110 g)	1.5
Chicken breast	1	1
Chicken leg	1	1
Tuna	3 oz (85 g)	1
Salmon	3 oz (85 g)	0.7

Source: The Gerontology Research Centre, Simon Fraser University

Counting Calories

Once you decide what to eat, the next step is to figure out how much. Depending on the amount and type of exercise you are doing, you may need to consume twice as many calories as you would if you were not exercising. If you want to maintain your present physique or build, you'll want to think about the "calories in, calories out" formula. Simply put, your physique will remain fairly con-

Pam

Pam was never the athletic type. She spent most of her adolescent school days dodging coaches who drooled at the thought of having her on the team. "I'm six-foot-two and my high-school gym teachers would weep for joy thinking about me with a basketball in my hand," recalls the 39-year-old public relations executive. "After they'd seen me in action, though, they'd shake their heads in disappointment and say, 'okay, you can go back to drama class now.' "

As an adult, she tagged along when a group of her friends decided to work through the 13-week walk/run program. She liked it and even excelled. Until then, she had never thought much about nutrition and was trying to figure out what was right when one member of her group had an "amazing" early-morning run after ingesting nothing more than coffee. "One day the next week I woke up late. I was really dragging my tail and I thought 'Hey, if it worked for Victoria, why not me?' " After enjoying an espresso at the local coffee shop, Pam joined her group. "I lasted about five minutes. I thought I was going to die," she recalls. "We were running over a bridge and I'm sure it was the hardest thing I'd ever done. Every step was a force of will. Honestly, had I been six years old I would have sat down on the curb and cried."

Pam feels she learned a valuable lesson that painful Saturday morning. "I learned that I have to get up and eat, which is kind of funny, considering I'd like to lose weight—I have all this extra fuel. Of course, it doesn't work that way." In addition to getting enough sleep the night before her run, Pam now takes it easy with alcohol the night before and treats herself to a decent pre-run meal. "Peanut butter on toast is good and cold pizza seems to work really well. One thing I know for sure is that for me, an espresso with sugar doesn't cut it!"

stant if the number of calories you take in equals the number of calories you burn doing work. (Keep in mind that you are constantly burning calories. You are burning calories reading this book and you are burning them when you sleep—not too many and not too fast, but burning them just the same.) If you take in more calories than you burn, they'll go into storage, usually as body fat. Take in fewer and you'll lose body fat.

Unfortunately, this is not always a perfect equation. Frustrated dieters know that eating less doesn't necessarily result in the loss of fat. If your body feels it is being deprived of energy, it will go into starvation mode and, at least to a certain extent, resist fat loss. It does this for evolutionary reasons—essentially because it doesn't know how long it's going to be until you'll start eating properly again. (More on losing weight later.)

If you want to get really specific about calories, visit a registered dietitian. You can get a complete analysis of your current diet and a program that will help you not only figure out what to eat, but how to plan your meals so that going to the supermarket isn't an exercise in frustration and dread.

Snacking

Snacking can be can be good for your diet, as long as you snack on the right things. Consider an apple rather than a candy bar, a glass of skim milk rather than a soda. Fresh fruit may seem to lack kick if you're accustomed to candy bars, but your taste buds will quickly adapt. Most people find that after a couple of weeks of changing such habits,

High-carbohydrate foods

The following moderate portions of high-carbohydrate foods are good sources of energy for runners.

- ½ cup (125 mL) raisins
- 4 Fig Newtons
- 1 energy bar
- 1 medium bagel
- 8 oz (250 mL) grape juice
- 1 medium banana
- 8 oz (250 mL) orange juice

natural foods seem wonderfully sweet and the sugary assault of artificial sources seems cloying. Sport energy bars should also be treated as a snack, not a meal, no matter what the manufacturers claim; they simply don't contain enough nutrients to qualify as a meal.

Pre-Training Nutrition

There are two reasons why you should eat before your training session. First, you want to have enough energy to do the work—gas in the tank. Second, when you're training you want to be thinking about training and how to get the most out of it, not about how hungry you are.

If you want to eat a full meal before your training session, make sure you give yourself enough time to digest it: three hours for a dinner-size meal and two hours for a smaller meal (compared with about an hour for a snack). Your body can do only so many large jobs at once, so if it's busy digesting a heavy meal it won't be very efficient at lifting heavy weights or running.

Pre-training meals help prevent low blood sugar (hypoglycemia) and its accompanying symptoms of fatigue, dizziness, blurred vision and indecisiveness, all of which can have you making the wrong choices even with something as benign as running. Ideally, your pre-training meal or snack should provide you with nutrients that are easily digested and help maintain the right fluid balance. It should include foods you are familiar with and enjoy eating, partly so you'll eat well and partly so your system won't have to tackle something it's not accustomed to—your body is trained by habit to digest certain foods, so the enzymes you produce to do the job are unique. Provided you give yourself enough time to digest it, your pre-training food can be anything from a traditional Thanksgiving dinner to tofu on rice, but the experts recommend you lean more toward the carbohydrate group because fat, protein and fiber all slow digestion.

Your training period is a good time to experiment with different eating habits to find what works for you. This is where a training log can be helpful: it can show you patterns of response based on eating habits.

Here are some pre-training food recommendations that have proven effective for many:

- Cold cereal, skim milk and a banana
- Hot cereal with brown sugar and applesauce
- Pasta with tomato sauce and a glass of skim milk
- Crackers, a little cheese and some fruit
- Whole wheat bread with peanut butter, some fruit and a glass of skim milk
- Low-fat yogurt, fresh fruit and graham wafers
- A liquid meal: blend a spoonful of low-fat yogurt, 1 cup (250 mL) of skim milk, a banana and 1 tsp (5 mL) of vanilla

Just Drink It

For a runner, water can be even more important than food. The human body is 70 per cent water and it loses water all the time through perspiration, respiration (breathing) and excretion. Perspiration is the body's natural air conditioning system: when you heat up the mechanism through exercise, you start to sweat more. To maintain

Many people have unrealistic expectations about how much weight they should lose and how fast they can lose it. A 154-lb (70-kg) woman walking 3½ miles (5.6 km) per hour would have to walk for approximately 16 hours to lose 1 lb (0.5 kg).

your fluid balance, you must drink enough to replace the water lost as sweat. Sometimes the loss is barely noticeable, and athletes can be shocked to discover they have run out of fluid. Skiers and people exercising in hot, dry climates are particularly vulnerable, as they often don't notice how much they are perspiring. Sometimes the signal is a stinging thirst that can't be allayed no matter how much water you consume. Have you ever had the experi-

Chas

Chas came to running for only one reason: he wanted to lose weight. The 35-year-old insurance adjuster explains, "The idea of being in shape and all that appealed, but not much. All I cared about was losing weight."

The idea of taking up running came to him at his 10-year high-school reunion. "I was looking at this guy I used to know and thinking, 'Boy, has he ever put on weight.' A little while later I went up to this girl I'd known and she looked at me like she didn't recognize me. I had to tell her my name and when I did she looked amazed. 'You turned out to be pretty big,' she said. I felt terrible."

Chas started going to a local gym, but riding stationary bikes and slogging away on stair-climbers left him cold. He complained about it to one of the attendants, who immediately suggested he join a running group. Running with other people would help with motivation and it would be a lot less boring than riding or running on the spot. It took Chas a while to get to the point where he could run for more than five minutes, but it was a lot more interesting than the gym.

Like most people who come to running in a panic, Chas hoped for instant results, and not getting them was discouraging. "It took me a while to learn that if I wanted to lose weight, I would have to do more than just run." Someone in his running group recommended some books on nutrition, and though it took Chas a while to change his habits, once he got his mind and diet in sync, the weight started to come off. "It's not like you'd see me in one of those diet commercials or anything, but my weight is going down and I'm pretty confident I can keep it going that way—hopefully until the next reunion anyway."

ence of suddenly getting thirsty, yet though you drank and drank until the water welled up in your belly, the thirst wouldn't go away? That happens because the "air conditioner" has run out of water and it takes time for your body to get the water you drink into the system again. This is why it's crucial for you to start drinking water early on in your workout, *before* you get thirsty.

There are other less obvious reasons to replace water lost through perspiration. Water filters out toxins, and helps the body digest food and turn it into a form that moves easily through the blood vessels. It also helps transmit electrical messages through the body.

So how much water do you need? Lots and lots. If you're not getting any exercise, the experts recommend six to eight glasses each day. If you're exercising, your requirements go up. How much they go up depends on how hard you're working out, the temperature around you and the clothing or equipment you're wearing. It's hard to drink too much water. As a rule, it's a good idea to start loading up on water well before you start exercising. Drink at least two glasses about two hours before you exercise and then another one or two about 15 minutes before you start to work out. Drink up to another glass every 15 to 20 minutes while you are exercising. Finally, don't stop when the training session ends: drink another one to three glasses within 10 to 20 minutes after you stop exercising.

Note that these are guidelines only; the commonly recommended amounts may not sufficiently hydrate some people. The only way to know if you are properly hydrated

 The human body is made up of 70 per cent water, and its need for water increases tremendously with exercise. That's because water is lost not just through perspiration, but also through increased breathing.

Fluid replacement guidelines

You need more water than you think. Here's a quick chart:

2 hours before exercise

2 cups (500 mL)

10–15 minutes before exercising

1–2 cups (250–500 mL)

Every 15–20 minutes during exercise

$1/3$–1 cup (75–250 mL)

10–20 minutes after exercise

1–3 cups (250–750 mL)

after intense exercise, especially when the weather is warm, is to weigh yourself before and after exercise, wearing the same clothes both times or, better yet, nothing at all. (If the sweat has soaked into your clothing, you'll get a false reading.) Weight lost during exercise represents water loss you did not replace during your workout.

Resist the urge to follow up your training session with alcohol. Although you'll often see athletes tilting a beer after a workout, mumbling something about having "earned it," alcohol is a diuretic and will only make your already thirsty body more dehydrated. (If you must have alcohol after your training session, at least try to down a few glasses of water at the same time.)

Of course, water isn't the only source of fluid you have to rely on. Most things you drink during the day will help meet your requirements. Coffee, however, isn't one of them. Like alcohol, it's a diuretic, and with added cream and sugar, it's a pretty unhealthy concoction. Fruit juices are okay, but avoid heavily sugared ones (and heavily sugared anything, for that matter) because too much sugar in your gut will draw water away from your muscles. When you run, this can cause further dehydration, leading to nausea, diarrhea and cramps.

Sport drinks are more than just marketing hype. Some of these drinks replace electrolytes such as salt and potassium; others provide the carbohydrates and sugars your body will crave in the middle of a long race. Some drinks will do both. These drinks may be useful for athletes competing in long-duration (more than two-hour-long), intense activities such as marathons or triathlons, or training for more than one and one half hours. For short-duration exercise—the type of training you'll be doing in the 13-week walk/run program—water will do just fine.

Weight Management

Seasoned runners tend to have a rather lean and hungry look, which is perhaps one reason so many people turn to running as a form of weight control. Although it's not an overnight cure, or even a short-term cure, running can be a remarkably effective aid to weight control. That said, becoming a runner requires patience and dedication. A lot of people who want to lose weight will try running and when they don't quickly get the results they were aiming for, give up. The fact is, it usually takes six months before the physiological benefits associated with running become noticeable, and about a year before a runner's body starts to look really different. Consider how long it took to put the weight on in the first place. Why should it take any less time to take it off?

It's also worth remembering that a regular running program will not lead to weight loss if you eat french fries for dinner every night. If you want to lose weight, you must stick to a balanced diet and get prolonged and regular aerobic exercise. There's no easy way, no machine, no pill.

If weight loss is your goal, try to remember that you were born with a certain type of body. Being rakishly thin may not be in your genes. Some people are thin by nature; others will never be thin, no matter how much exercise they do. This does not mean that those people can't shed excess poundage, but be realistic about how much weight you are going to be able to lose and from what part of your body the fat will be lost. That "spare tire" of body fat

Water is the perfect lubricant for your body. It is 100 per cent natural, low in sodium and has no fat. The colour of your urine can show whether you're drinking enough: clear-colored urine is a sign you are probably sufficiently hydrated; dark-colored urine means you should probably be drinking more.

Helpful hints for managing your weight

- No single weight-control prescription is ideal for everyone
- Exercise at moderate intensity for 25–45 minutes, 3–4 times each week
- To increase the rate of fat loss, gradually increase exercise duration
- Try to include strength training twice a week to increase muscle mass (muscle burns more calories even at rest than do other body tissues)
- Wait at least 6 months before assessing physiological changes such as improved cardiovascular fitness and increased muscle strength
- Expect it to take 6–9 months for your body's proportion of fat to decrease measurably as a result of exercise

around your middle will be a lot easier to lose through exercise than will fat on your hips and thighs, because fat located around the hips and thighs is controlled by reproductive hormones rather than stress hormones and is more closely protected by the body.

If you've been sedentary, it's important to start with lower-intensity exercise and progressively build up to a moderate- to high-intensity level, which is what the 13-week program does. Once you have achieved a higher fitness level, however, running at lower speeds will no longer be the best way to burn fat or achieve fat loss. Working at moderate- to high-intensity levels in either one 40- to 60-minute session or a number of shorter sessions per training day will burn more total calories and ultimately more fat.

One last warning: beware of fad diets. Fad diets are invariably designed to capitalize on people's insecurities and to make money for their developers, not to improve the health of the people who follow them. This is not to say that all diets are to be mistrusted, just that there's no magic to good nutrition. If you use the tools of good nutrition, chances are you won't need to search for miracle cures.

If you want more detailed information about weight loss—or about diet, nutrition or menu planning—check out some of the useful sources listed at the back of this book.

Common Injuries & Recovery

INJURIES ARE NOT ONLY PAINFUL, THEY'RE DISCOURAGING. If, after putting in countless hours building up your endurance, you get an injury that prevents you from running, you have to sit idly by and watch as the fitness level you worked so hard to attain slowly slips away. If running is your main outlet for managing stress, you may feel especially frustrated and angry, and may even be tempted to dull the pain of injury with painkillers and try to carry on. This is the time to remember that injuries ignored are injuries that can haunt you for a lifetime.

Although it's true the 13-week walk/run program is designed to minimize your chances of suffering a running-related injury, you can still be sidelined—as a result of an accident, overzealous training or your own biomechanical weaknesses. To remain healthy, it's essential to understand the kinds of injuries runners are susceptible to and the treatments offering the best chance for a full and complete recovery.

Types of Injuries

There are two major categories of injuries that runners should think about, says Hugh Fisher, a family practitioner and Olympic gold and

During a mile (1.61 kilometers) of running, your foot strikes the ground between 800 and 1,200 times (500 to 750 times per kilometer) with a force of up to four times your body weight (the exact force depends on your speed and length of stride).

bronze medallist in kayaking/canoeing. Fisher has had his own litany of aches and pains over the years, and he's also seen plenty of sufferers struggling into his office.

The first category of injury is the acute kind, which can sneak up on anybody. Such injuries are usually "traumatic," the result of sudden and violent damage such as a torn ligament (sprain), laceration (cut), pulled muscle (sprain) or broken bone. Traumatic injuries are best treated as quickly as possible by a qualified sport medicine practitioner, especially if there's any bleeding, a good deal of swelling or pain that lasts more than an hour. You should also attend to an injury quickly if you find it so debilitating that you can't walk or make use of the injured body part, or if you heard, or hear, any unusual sounds—popping, cracking or tearing.

Runners' traumatic injuries are most often caused by falls, from tripping over roots, curbs and the like. Unfortunately, the most interesting places to run are to blame for the most accidents. Trail running is extremely popular but the unevenness of the terrain and the looseness of the ground often results in falls. Trail runners need to keep their eyes on the surface beneath them if that surface is uneven, and be extra cautious about footwear. Shoes that don't fit or that lack adequate support increase a runner's risk of taking a spill.

The second category of running injuries—by far the more common—is overuse, or chronic injury that results from overtraining. Sometimes chronic injuries can be traced back to poor technique, but this is rare in beginning runners, who run neither fast enough nor far enough for technique-related problems to develop (but see the advice on running technique in Chapter 6 if you want more information about this possibility). "Overuse injuries often show up in people who are extremely competitive by nature," says Fisher. "They train every day and never give their bodies a chance to rest. Muscle and joint injuries are common, but sickness can also result, because they are just generally run down."

Dr. Jim Macintyre, a sport physician in Salt Lake City, Utah, says many overuse injuries result either from incomplete rehabilitation of an old injury, or from individual anatomical variations that lead to injury when put under stress. These variations can include flat feet, high arches or an abnormally sized or positioned kneecap. The results are the same: when there's a weak link in the kinetic (moving) chain—some part that's out of alignment naturally or as the result of an injury—the body compensates for that weakness to keep the person going. This usually leads to a different, new injury. For Macintyre, the red flags go up when athletes come to him suffering from a cycle of injuries to one side of their body. First it's the right ankle, then the right knee, then perhaps the right hip.

"Think about it," urges Macintyre. "How many people come in with one knee sore versus both knees sore? The mantra is to say it's the shoes, lack of flexibility, poor training methods, bad running techniques and so on. But generally, people wear the same shoes on both feet and run the same number of steps with both legs—give or take one or two—so how can you blame the shoes when you have only one sore knee?"

Keep a logbook

Maintaining a logbook will help you track the origin of any injuries. For every injury I've had, I can look back in my logbook and usually pinpoint the "Why?" It's often something I've forgotten about, like tripping over a branch.

- Note the workout, time of day, how you fell, special conditions (you were up all night before your run with sick kids, for example)
- Keep it simple
- Be honest

—*Olympian Lynn Kanuka*

It's not that the injury can't be the result of the wrong shoes, poor flexibility, unsound training methods or bad technique, but that often the knees, heels, ankles and other sensitive links in the kinetic chain are the victims, not the culprits—the source of the injury lies elsewhere. For this reason, Macintyre, along with many other practitioners, recommends that doctors look at the whole body, not only when it's lying supine on a plinth in the doctor's office, but when it's in motion as well. Macintyre likes to see his patients walking and even running on treadmills to see how their whole body moves and where the trouble they're experiencing might originate. "You have to look at the whole chain. You look at the foot, you look at the hip and you look at the pelvis. You watch them walk and you watch them run," Macintyre says.

Tracking down the source of an injury is a bit of a detective game, according to Macintyre. "As a health care

RUNNER PROFILE

Helen

Helen, 49, was trying to increase her running endurance in preparation for a race when she got a surprise visit from an old enemy. "I dislocated my knee when I was in ballet," says the retired aerobics instructor, who now works as an office administrator. "When I tried to increase the time I spent running, it was too much." Her weakened knee could take only so much stress before it gave out and she developed patello-femoral syndrome (runner's knee).

Wisely, considering the severity of her injury, Helen's first instincts were the best ones: she cut out the running and went to see a doctor. His rehabilitation program returned her to running in less than a month, but only for 10 minutes at a time, so her knee injury didn't flare up again. "He recommended a stretching and strengthening program and I also got orthotics. He keeps testing the knee to make sure it was holding out. With the last test he had me using a skipping rope, and I didn't have any pain, so I guess I passed."

In a few months, Helen was back up to running for 30 minutes at a stretch, but she continued her stretching and strengthening program because she had her sights set on a half marathon.

professional, the question you have to ask yourself is: Why did they get this pain, and why in one knee and not the other? The obvious answer is that there must be something intrinsically imbalanced about the patient's gait. One possibility is that they're running on a sloped road surface. One leg is forced into a shortened position while the other leg lengthens, forcing the foot to pronate excessively. The knee becomes the victim in the whole thing. It has had abnormal amounts of stress placed on it as a result of something somewhere else that's causing the abnormal gait. It could also be something as simple as a foot that's not moving properly, a hip that's tight or a pelvis that's out of place due to a problem with the sacroiliac joint."

For example, in a properly aligned body, the kneecap should track evenly over the foot in a straight line pointing in the direction you are traveling. If something—such as a misaligned hip—causes your knee to track in another direction, your knee will eventually be injured, and you won't even think about it until enough damage has been done for the knee to send pain signals to your brain. To make matters worse, if you, your doctor or your physiotherapist don't figure out the root cause of the injury, the knee will be treated and you'll go back to running as soon as it feels better. Then, guess what? The knee will be injured again. "To tell someone they have a bad knee when they come to you with knee pain is simply not good enough. If all you're going to try to do is identify the symptoms, then you say, 'Okay, this is patello-femoral pain,' you get out your cookbook and it says 'ice it, take anti-inflammatories and do these exercises.' But all you're treating are the symptoms, not the cause of the problem."

Injury prevention

- Always wear the proper gear, including suitable shoes
- Don't push yourself too hard—stick with your training schedule
- Promptly attend to injuries—use the RICE treatment and get a medical evaluation if the injury seems serious or if pain persists
- Modify your training when injured or ill—don't try to "run through" an injury or "run out" an illness
- Take care when returning to training after an injury or illness—follow professional advice
- Don't ignore pain

Tips for cold-weather running

- If there is ice on the road, slow down your run so that you don't get injured
- Keep warm by including a hat, gloves and a windbreaker as part of your gear
- Layer your clothes so that you can better regulate your body temperature
- Keep moving; standing still will cause you to cool down quickly

Sometimes the pain migrates to a different part of your body—your ankle or your Achilles tendon. Why? During treatment you probably did exercises that strengthened the muscles around your bad knee, giving it a greater ability to compensate for the problem that could be originating in your hip. The flaw then migrates to the next weakest link in the chain, then the next and so on.

New injuries can also be caused by old injuries that haven't healed properly. An old ankle sprain, for example, might lock one foot into pronation while the other supinates (rolls outward). Macintyre says he's looked at thousands of people with one pronated foot and one supinated foot and at first thought it odd these people were born like that. "But the truth is, they weren't born like that. Somewhere along the way something happened to the ankle that changed the range of motion or flexibility. The alignment was thrown out of balance and the rest of the links in the chain started to compensate. Before the person started running, they may never have noticed this. There wasn't enough stress being put on various parts of their body for them to break down, but the stresses associated with running revealed the inherent weaknesses."

Biomechanical problems are not an absolute guarantee that an injury will manifest itself. Everyone's body has some ability to compensate: sometimes your body parts are strong enough to compensate forever. If, on the other hand, you exceed your body's ability to compensate, injury is headed your way.

Sadly, some runners get into a cycle of injuries and eventually throw in the towel. "I used to run," you'll hear them say miserably, "but my [fill-in-the-blank] couldn't take it." Maybe it couldn't, but more likely, these runners didn't follow the right course of treatment. If you do get a running injury, know when you're out of your league and if you don't see fairly rapid improvement from self-treatment, get help from a professional who understands sports injuries. Sport medicine is not a strict discipline the way cardiology or neurology is, but an increasing number of medical practitioners focus on sports-related injuries. These practitioners include orthopedic surgeons, family physicians (such as Hugh Fisher) and sport medicine specialists (such as Jim Macintyre). Other practitioners who may focus on sport-related injuries include podiatrists, chiropractors, physiotherapists, athletic therapists, athletic trainers and massage therapists. You want someone who will examine the entire chain of your moving parts, someone who can assess the body in motion and not just look at localized pain.

If you are told to rest the injured part and just wait for the pain to go away, you may want to seek a second opinion. If the cause of your pain isn't treated, chances are the pain will come back when you start running again. An experienced sport medicine practitioner can both give a diagnosis and prescribe a treatment regimen, which will probably include alternative activities and a program of strength and flexibility training. By and large, you will find that sport medicine is more "aggressive" than traditional medicine in its treatment plan.

Tips for hot-weather running

- Slow down your run
- Protect yourself from the sun by wearing a mesh hat and applying sunblock
- Wear a light-colored or white shirt made of a synthetic material; it will keep you cool by moving sweat away from your body
- Drink more water than usual before, during and after a run
- Run at cooler times during the day, such as in the early morning or in the evening
- Run on forest trails, for protection from the sun in summer—from the cold and rain in winter
- Plan a route that takes you through a kids' water park

Managing an acute injury

If you've been injured, remember the word RICE as a guideline for what you should do.

- Rest or restrict activity until an accurate diagnosis can be made
- Ice the injury for 20 minutes per hour as often as possible for the first 24–48 hours
- Compress the injury with an elastic tension bandage (but never too tightly or for too long)
- Elevate the injured area above the level of the heart

Runner's First Aid

If you are injured, you should seek medical attention. While you're waiting for help, however, you can get started on RICE. The acronym RICE stands for Rest, Ice, Compression and Elevation. It's standard procedure; everybody does it because it works.

RICE is often used in conjunction with anti-inflammatory drugs such as acetylsalicylic acid/ASA (Aspirin) or ibuprofen (Advil or Motrin). These drugs can reduce swelling but should not be relied upon as a crutch to mask pain and allow you to "run through" injuries. Also, remember that ASA and ibuprofen can be hard on your stomach, so take them with food. Note that although acetaminophen (Tylenol) is easier on the stomach and an effective painkiller, it is not an anti-inflammatory and will not reduce swelling.

Rest

The reason for rest is straightforward: if you've damaged something, putting more stress on it can only make it worse. But taking things easy doesn't mean you have to spend three weeks on the couch watching TV before you can use the injured part. Complete immobility is rarely recommended, the possible exception being in acute traumatic cases, and even then doctors will try to get you up and moving as soon as possible.

Moving injured parts is important because it stimulates blood flow to the injured soft tissue. In fact, anything that stimulates blood flow will encourage healing, which is why so many physiotherapists use ultrasound and similar stimulation techniques. Most of the time, however, unless you get in the way, your body's own healing powers will regenerate and restore damaged soft tissue.

A sport medicine practitioner will often recommend certain exercises to go along with RICE. These are usually designed to strengthen the muscles around the injury in order to help your body compensate. By strengthening the muscles around a vital part, such as the knee, you can support that part and make it easier for it to do its job. Exercises can also be designed to increase flexibility and enhance circulation, thereby spurring on the natural healing process. So do your exercises; they will make it easier for you to withstand the stress of returning to your activity because you will be stronger and more flexible than when you were injured in the first place.

Ice

You've no doubt noticed that swelling occurs when you injure yourself. This swelling is actually part of the healing process. It may seem contradictory, but even though swelling is part of the healing process, too much of it slows healing. Applying ice causes what is known as vasoconstriction of the local blood vessels in the area surrounding the injury, which limits bleeding and thereby reduces swelling in the area.

By reducing swelling, icing reduces the recovery time, so the sooner you can ice an injury the better. Obviously you won't always have an ice pack with you when you run, but in an emergency, cold water will help immensely. If you're desperate, use the water from your water bottle to soak your T-shirt and wrap the injury. If you can, hold the injured part under cold water until you can find some ice and properly apply it.

Just ice it!

- I don't always have an ice pack… a bag of frozen peas or corn can be held equally well on an injury
- Fill Styrofoam cups with water, and when you need to ice your injury before exercising, peel back the Styrofoam and use the ice to massage the injured area

—Olympian Lynn Kanuka

When you apply ice, do so for approximately 20 minutes at a time, allowing at least an hour between treatments. Repeat this as often as possible for the first 24 to 72 hours. Loading ice into plastic bags is fine, but having soft-pack ice bags in the freezer is markedly more efficient, not to mention a lot less messy. Soft-packs tend to warm up quickly when they contact inflamed skin and joints, but if you have several, you can just keep rotating them. Be careful when applying ice near sensitive nerves (such as those of the spine, or at the back of the knee) or important organs like the eyes and heart.

As well, don't make the mistake of icing something, then following up with a hot bath, which will actually open up the blood vessels and increase swelling.

Compression

Compression—achieved with an elastic bandage—helps reduce swelling, pain and bruising and hasten the healing

Dennis and Rosario

At the age of 30, Dennis was too sedentary, and he knew it, says his wife, Rosario. "He's a programmer/analyst, spending all his time sitting in front of a computer screen. He was going everywhere by car, so I was getting kind of concerned." The two of them decided to follow the 13-week walk/run program.

Because he had not exercised for a long time, even this moderate program left Dennis feeling sharp pains in his calf muscles. Luckily, Dennis and Rosario attended a training-program seminar where the lecturer focused on warming up and cooling down, and explained what a difference shoes could make. "So we went out right away and each bought a good pair of shoes," Rosario says. At the same time, Dennis and Rosario added warm-ups and cool-downs to their routine. The results were impressive. Both of them are running completely free of pain.

process, especially when combined with ice and elevation. If you're self-doctoring with an elastic bandage, don't overdo the tension. A compression bandage should be left on for no longer than three hours, unless you are following the advice of a qualified professional. It should never be left on overnight.

Elevation

Elevation serves two purposes. If your foot or another injured body part is elevated, you're not walking around or running on it (see "Rest," page 132). More important, however, at least in the short term, when your injured extremity is above your heart there is less pooling of the blood and therefore less swelling. As with ice, when it comes to elevation, sooner is better.

Common Injuries

By following the 13-week walk/run program, giving sufficient time to warming up and cooling down, watching where you are going and investing in proper footwear, not to mention feeding your body properly and keeping it hydrated, you are going a long way toward preventing injury. Nevertheless, on the theory that it's best to be prepared, the following are parts of the body most commonly affected by running-related injury (the list is from Dr. Tim Noakes and is arranged from the most to the least frequent site of injury):

- Attachment of ligament to bone and tendon to bone
- Bones
- Muscles
- Tendons

 Heat should never be applied to an injury until swelling has subsided. It can increase blood flow to the injured area, thereby increasing the swelling and possibly tissue damage as well.

- Bursae (the fluid-filled sacs between tendons and bones that allow for free movement of tendons over bones)
- Blood vessels (both arteries and veins)
- Nerves

Within this wide range of possibilities are half a dozen injuries sport medicine practicioners are most commonly called upon to treat, summarized here for your convenience.

Patello-femoral syndrome

Also known as runner's knee (a term coined in the 1970s by running guru and author Dr. George Sheehan), patello-femoral syndrome is characterized by some very specific symptoms, including:

- localized pain around the kneecap that is not the result of sudden trauma;
- pain in the knee that gets worse over time and often manifests itself after a certain distance;
- pain that comes on if the knee is bent and immobile for a certain period of time, such as when you're sitting in a movie theater.

Runner's knee is a huge problem and accounts for about a quarter of all visits to sport medicine clinics. It is a classic overuse injury and occurs at the inner or outer border of the kneecap. Noakes says runner's knee is most commonly caused by excessive ankle pronation (inward rotation of the foot). The foot itself may be at fault, or it may be compensating for an abnormality elsewhere. In any case, the excessive pronation causes a twisting force at the knee, pulling the kneecap out of its correct alignment. Keep pulling on it long enough and you will be looking for ice packs and an aisle seat next time you go to the movies.

Short-term treatment for runner's knee includes the RICE technique, but you can heal it in the long term only if you correct the underlying biomechanical problems causing it. Some doctors may advise surgery; you are well advised to get a second opinion if this treatment is recommended to you.

One way to correct overpronation is to work with your footwear to prevent the foot from twisting. Sometimes a more supportive and/or differently shaped shoe can make a difference; some people need the further help of orthotics (customized foot supports). Orthotics play an important role and they should be prescribed and built by trained experts. Consult with your doctor or podiatrist about this option.

Iliotibial band syndrome

Runner's knee isn't the only injury that can affect your knees. The iliotibial band is a strip of connective tissue that runs from the hip down the outside of the leg to just below the knee, where it is inserted into the outside of the tibia (shin bone). Repeated bending and straightening of the knee, combined with biomechanical weaknesses, can lead to this connective tissue becoming irritated as it rubs back and forth over the bony outside of the knee, a protuberance known as the femoral condyle. If you've ever

A study reported in the *American Journal of Sport Medicine* in 1996 showed that running strengthens the joints by improving muscle tone, increasing bone density and increasing the amount of synovial (lubricating) fluid.

had this happen, you can talk with some authority about what it might be like to get shot in the knee: this injury can be extremely painful. In general, the pain may go away with rest but comes on with relentless fury during exercise, when movement causes the iliotibial band to cross the femoral condyle.

Poor shoes, hard running surfaces and training errors have all been cited as possible causes of iliotibial band syndrome, but Macintyre claims it's often a compensatory injury. Noakes agrees, having found that about 70 per cent of sufferers have biomechanical structures that inadequately absorb shock. These structures include bow-legs, high arches and rigid feet.

RICE is a good local treatment, but long-term treatment should include softer shoes that can better absorb shock. Avoid hard running surfaces, and cambered roads and hills, both up and down. A good warm-up and stretching program is crucial to prevent (or recover from) iliotibial band syndrome, and gradual adjustments to your training routine may also be required.

If this condition comes on suddenly, ask yourself if you're doing something you didn't do before. Did you change your running route? Did you just buy new shoes? If so, go back to the old way for a while and see if it makes a difference.

Plantar fasciitis

Plantar fasciitis is less common than iliotibial band syndrome and runner's knee, but it's a pain in the foot for those who get it. Patients commonly complain of what feels like a bruised heel; putting pressure on it hurts.

Actually, the heel itself is not the problem. The plantar fascia is a band of connective tissue running from the heel to the toes; trouble can occur where it attaches to the heel. People who suffer from plantar fasciitis have difficulty when running and when getting out of bed in the morning. You can spot them walking stiffly, because when they put their full weight on their foot the arch stretches out and causes pain.

Plantar fasciitis is thought to be caused by the same thing as runner's knee—excessive pronation. It also tends to occur more commonly in people with high arches. Research so far indicates that overly stiff shoes can exacerbate the condition, as can a sudden increase in the frequency or intensity of training. Plantar fasciitis is a classic overuse injury and if you get it, it's a sign that your training may be progressing too fast. Although the 13-week walk/run program is paced to avoid injury, it may be too much for some people. If you get plantar fasciitis while following the prescribed program, you may be one of them. If that's the case, you will need to back off and take a more gradual approach.

Treatment for plantar fasciitis includes RICE. Consider your footwear carefully; try a softer shoe or perhaps orthotics. Also, try running on softer surfaces. Strengthening and stretching can help. Work on your quadriceps (the big muscles at the front of your upper leg), calf muscles and the small muscles in your feet.

Achilles tendinitis

The Achilles tendon is named for an ancient Greek hero who was considered invulnerable. At birth, his mother dipped him in a special bath that made his skin impregnable. The problem was, she held him by the heel to do it, so that part of his body didn't get the benefit of the magic solution. Achilles went down in the Trojan War when an enemy spear severed the seemingly unimportant tendon running from his calf muscles to his heel. Ever since the poet Homer first immortalized Achilles, the story of his tendon has been used as a metaphor for the weak link in a seemingly impregnable chain. As it turns out, you don't need to sever this tendon to be out of action: a little inflammation—that is, Achilles tendinitis—will do the trick.

RUNNER PROFILE

Vince

Vince, 50, a writer, had spent a lifetime indulging in sports, but his endurance needed a boost. Running seemed like the perfect way to increase his cardiovascular conditioning; he reckoned it would make him an even better tennis player and help him keep up with his opponents, all of whom seemed to be getting younger every year.

Slowly, though, running took over. "It did build up my endurance, but I came to enjoy it for its own sake. It's nice to go from a sport where you're very competitive all the time and where intimidation is such a factor to one where you're competing only against yourself. I like the idea that you can do it at your own pace and you don't have to worry about having the right facilities, or opponents or anything."

Then Vince started having shooting pains in his feet. The diagnosis was stress fractures. Fortunately, instead of trying to run through the pain—perhaps loading up on painkillers and hoping the problem would just go away—Vince changed his program and rehabilitated his feet. "I took some time off, went over to cycling for a while and started a stretching program." He also avoided running on concrete, opting for soft tracks and park trails instead. As a result, Vince is now back to running three times a week for 40 minutes at a stretch.

Damage to the Achilles tendon can occur quickly, as it did with our Greek hero, or over time, as it usually does with runners. Sufferers first notice a prickly or burning sensation, followed later by a more acute, shooting pain that is especially noticeable when they change direction or run uphill. Over time, the collagen protein fibers of the tendon can break down and the results can be catastrophic—the tendon may actually snap or rupture. The pain is, as you can imagine, remarkable.

The Achilles tendon is particularly vulnerable as it has a poor blood supply to the area that is more often affected. Add excessive ankle pronation, which tends to cause a whipping action, and the result is tendinitis. Other contributing causes can include constant rubbing of the shoe against the tendon, insufficient warm-up, poor shoe quality or fit, trauma and some kind of heel-bone deformity.

Treatment includes RICE and trying a more stable shoe that controls foot motion. Orthotics can help, as can working to increase the flexibility and strength of your feet, calves and shins. Don't be reluctant to take this complaint to a doctor; an untreated Achilles injury can have lasting implications.

Tibial stress syndrome

Sometimes incorrectly referred to as shin splints, tibial stress syndrome is usually caused by minute tears in the muscles where they attach to the shin. The damage can occur in any of three places: anterior (at the front of the tibia—the big bone in your lower leg), posterior (at the back of the tibia) or laterally (along the fibula—the smaller bone in your lower leg). Numerous explanations for these injuries have been put forth, including tightness in the muscles, for which the traditional cure was surgery. Today, researchers blame excessive pronation or too much shock to the bone from repeatedly applied stress. Inadequate flexibility in the ankle—an old injury?—could also be the cause.

Treatment includes RICE, cutting back on running for a time (listen to your body—one to two weeks should do it), orthotics, and stretching and strengthening the muscles in the lower leg. Avoid overstriding while running and make sure your shoes provide you with good support and cushioning.

Stress fractures

Stress fractures are very small, incomplete breaks or cracks in bones that result from repeated stress or pounding. Bones repair themselves, of course, but if you knock away at them faster than they can regenerate they will deteriorate. You can get stress fractures just about anywhere, but runners generally get them in their shins and/or feet. And it's not just small bones that are susceptible; stress fractures in the hip are also possible.

Although repeated pounding is the most common cause of stress fractures, you can also pave the way for them by cheating your body of the nutritional elements it needs to carry on the important job of bone building (see Chapter 7, Fueling the Body). Stress fractures do not generally show up on X-rays until healing is well underway. Your doctor *may* order a bone scan to help make the diagnosis, but a physical exam is often sufficient. The key sign of a stress fracture is acute pain that can be pinpointed to a specific area.

Treatment includes RICE and switching away from whatever activity is causing the damage until sufficient healing has taken place to allow a return to that activity. Casting is almost never recommended, though depending on the site and the seriousness of the fracture, immobilization (using crutches) may be an option. Stress fractures can be serious if not treated early and well; deal with them when they first present themselves and you will get back to running sooner. To prevent stress fractures, avoid running on hard surfaces and make sure you have the right shoes for your feet.

Delayed Onset Muscle Soreness (DOMS)

It is not uncommon to feel stiff and sore after you exercise, if you try a new activity or start up again after some time away from it. "Delayed onset muscle soreness, or DOMS," explains Dr. Jim Macintyre, "is caused by microtrauma to tiny blood vessels as a result of an unaccustomed amount of exercise. The trauma causes the blood vessels to leak and fluid to accumulate." The soreness indicates that you are trying to do too much too soon. Exercise gently until the soreness and swelling decrease, and stretch, cool the affected muscles and elevate your legs.

Coming Back

Not everyone who takes up running gets a running injury, and if you do, you don't necessarily have to stop training until you are completely healed. Provided your doctor

Getting back into action

If you're returning to exercise after illness or an injury, keep in mind the following precautions.

- Ensure that you have a pain-free range of motion in the injured area
- Be certain that the strength, endurance and coordination of the injured area is equal to that of the un-injured side (or at least is back to pre-injury levels)
- Start slowly and build back gradually
- Follow your doctor's advice

doesn't object, there are a variety of low-impact aerobic activities you can do while injured that will help keep you in the shape to which you have become accustomed. These can include rowing, swimming, pool running, cycling, cross-country skiing or even walking. And if you treat your injuries properly, most will heal in three to four weeks (longer for stress fractures) and you can return to your regular routine.

Don't return to running too soon, however. You want to come back gradually. If you were halfway through the program when you were sidelined and you've now been off for any length of time, consider starting from the beginning. Starting over may not sound like much fun, but remember that elite athletes frequently use a program very much like the 13-week walk/run program when they are returning from injury layoffs. One general rule is to never increase your activity level by more than 10 per cent

RUNNER PROFILE

Ian

Ian is a 54-year-old engineer and triathlete who runs an average of four times a week. Last year he tore his calf muscle during a hard run. After consulting with his sport medicine practitioner, Ian believes that his injury was due to a combination of dehydration and an extremely strenuous running workout.

Initially Ian was pretty upset about his injury, but, after speaking with his doctor and others in the triathlon community, he was confident that after a month or so of rehabilitation and rest he would be able to gradually resume running. Ian had previous experience with injuries and knew that if he wanted to maintain his cardiovascular fitness and positive mental attitude, he would have to replace running with another activity. As a triathlete, he chose to increase his number of bike and swim sessions each week. Weekly sessions with a physiotherapist were also integral to Ian's rehabilitation program.

After a month away from running, Ian was able to go for an easy jog. By modifying distance and speed over the course of two months, he was able to gradually return to his pre-injury running regimen.

(time or distance) per week. Follow your doctor's advice, and keep the following cautions in mind before resuming your running program:

- ensure that you have a pain-free range of motion in the injured area;

- check that the injured side of your body is equal—in terms of strength, endurance, coordination and speed of movement—to your uninjured side, or at least that it performs as well as it did before you were injured.

- ensure that you are psychologically prepared to return to running and confident you will not be re-injured.

Keep in mind that the injuries discussed in this chapter are only the most common ones runners can acquire. There are others. Pay attention to your aches and pains, and seek the advice of a qualified sport medicine practitioner if you have any concerns. Getting in shape is a good thing; hurting or damaging your body in pursuit of this goal is not.

Psychological effects of injuries

Up to this point, we have focused our attention on the physical aspects of rehabilitation from injury. For until recently, much of the focus in sport medicine has been on athletes' *physical* readiness to return to running. However, an injury that effects—or stops—you from running can also be a highly emotional experience, one that disrupts your mental health and well-being. And increasingly, medical practitioners are recognizing the importance of helping runners and regular exercisers cope with the psychological effects of their injuries. Without acknowledging and treating the emotional side of an injury, they know they are addressing only part of the problem.

Mind over injury?

- Someone who exercises regularly performs at a higher level throughout the day

- If an activity is eliminated, less oxygen is delivered to the brain than the runner is used to, and they perform at a lower level than before the injury

- Injured runners report disturbed sleep patterns

- Patience is often reduced

- Injured runners need to be aware that they won't feel as good as they did when they were exercising regularly

- When injured, runners need to find other fitness activities to enjoy, to preserve emotional well-being.

How a person reacts and later deals with an injury varies according to the individual. According to sport psychologist Dr. David Cox, anyone who runs regularly or who has a regular exercise regime will endure a sometimes lengthy adjustment period after an injury when they are unable to perform at their best. Many psychologists believe there are five stages in this adjustment period: denial and isolation, anger, bargaining, depression and acceptance. As Dr. Cox notes, "This model can be useful in anticipating emotional reactions to injury."

Staying active while injured

For various reasons, some of which have been identified earlier, it is important to stay active while injured. One way is with cross training—a great way to maintain strength and cardio fitness while injured. Cross training also helps

RUNNER PROFILE

Lynn

Lynn is a former Canadian Olympian and bronze-medal winner in the 3,000 meters at 1984's Los Angeles Olympics. Over the years, Lynn has overcome illiotibial band syndrome and numerous stress fractures. Leading up to the L.A. Olympics, Lynn was again plagued by a stress fracture that left her unable to run. She was devastated.

"During previous periods of injury, I cross trained using swimming and cycling to maintain fitness. While these activities left me aerobically fit, I was exercising different muscles from those used in running. Each time I returned to running, I felt awkward and more muscle-bound than before. So when it was suggested that I try running in water (keeping afloat in deep water by using my arms and legs the way I do when I run), I was open to it."

With Lynn's sights on the Olympic Games, she was determined to make her new training regimen work. At first she found it difficult to adapt, but after a few weeks she developed a comfortable and effective technique. Lynn trained exclusively in the water for eight weeks before she ran again on land. Four weeks after coming out of the pool, she ran a personal best in the 3,000 meters and set a new Canadian record.

"To many people this was unexplainable, but I knew exactly what accounted for it—running in water."

fight the injury blues, which are all too common.

For anyone who has been forced to take a break from running, or who has lived with someone in this situation, being sidelined with an injury can be fraught with frustration. But it doesn't have to be this way. Recovering from an injury can be seen as an opportunity to try a new activity and to strengthen areas of the body you may have otherwise neglected. If you cross train while injured, it's also likely you will be more patient and able to take a more gradual approach to returning to running. Starting back too soon or too quickly, because you're anxious about losing fitness or gaining weight, regularly results in re-injury.

Pool running

Besides swimming, cycling and walking, why not try pool running? It may not seem like the most exciting activity, but running in a pool is a great way to stay fit while nursing an injury. It's also a safe and effective way to add an extra run to your schedule and to avoid over-use injuries common to increases in running time and intensity.

Tips for running in water

The idea with pool running is to develop a proper running technique—using quick turnover of your arms and legs to allow you to stay afloat and move from one end of the pool to the other. It is not a race to get to the other end, but it is not a walk in the water, either. As you develop your technique:

- Try to mirror your running gate
- Avoid a bicycle movement with your legs—extend your quadriceps forward rather than upward, and

Tips for injured runners

- Seek out positive relationships with empathetic and supportive caregivers
- Educate yourself as to the nature of your injury and the expected course of recovery
- Develop a rehabilitation program
- Learn helpful psychological skills, such as goal setting, relaxation, positive self-talk and imagery
- Prepare yourself for possible setbacks and/or unexpected developments in your recovery

focus on pulling strongly back through the water with the hamstrings

- Maintain an upright position and avoid leaning forward too much
- Keep your head comfortably above water
- Avoid dog-paddling; keep your shoulders relaxed and move your arms straight forward and backward in the water
- Break the surface of the water in front with the fingertips and in back with the elbows... a strong arm action is very helpful
- Concentrate on keeping your elbows close to your body (to avoid a sideways motion)

RUNNER PROFILE

Jack

Jack is a sport medicine practitioner and an elite athlete who has represented Canada at numerous international events. By age 52, he had run more than 100,000 miles (161,000 kilometers) and competed in 60-plus marathons and ultra marathons. He was running an average of 80 miles (129 kilometers) a week and cycling regularly when he collapsed 18 miles (30 kilometers) into a long run. He required four-vessel coronary artery bypass surgery.

After returning home from the hospital, Jack says, "I walked a block and it felt like I had just walked a marathon. Initially, I restricted my exercise to walking. I had also suffered a mild stroke while in the hospital, which disrupted my balance, so biking was not an option." Instead Jack walked every day, gradually building up his pace and distance so that he was eventually able to complete a 1.5-hour walk at a brisk pace.

Two years later, he was back to running regularly. "Before I was a competitive runner, but now I run for my health. Running is what saved me. I approached my rehabilitation in the same way an athlete does when recovering from a knee injury. It wasn't my knee that I was trying to repair, but my body's most important muscle [the heart]. But I still used the same concept, the walk/run program, which I would prescribe to any athlete or regular exerciser wanting to return to running post-injury."

Returning to Running After a Significant Medical Problem

If you want to return to running after suffering a significant medical problem such as a heart attack, hip replacement surgery or cancer, it's essential to do so under the direction of your health care provider. Even if you were a regular exerciser prior to your health problems, it is important to heed the advice of your doctor.

The following are some commonly asked running-related questions from people wanting to know if—and how—they can return to running, with responses from sport medicine specialist Dr. Jack Taunton.

Q: *Can I return to running after my injury?*
A: For someone who is recovering from a significant medical problem, such as hip replacement surgery, or who is constantly plagued with sore knees, running may not be the best activity to take up again after an injury. Rather, walking, swimming or cycling may be better options.

Q: *I consistently have sore knees, even though I wear proper shoes and have been correctly fitted for orthotics. Can I begin a running program again or should I try another sport?*
A: Before giving up on running, try building up your quadricep strength with drop squats, then build up gradually through the walk/run program.

Q: *I recently underwent hip replacement surgery. Will I ever be able to return to a regular running routine?*
A: No, not if you want your hip to last a long time. It's important that you try another sport, such as cycling or swimming.

After an injury

- Take it *slow and easy,* with a regimen like the 13-week walk/run program on page 151
- Wait until you have been pain free for at least a week before making any attempt to run again
- If you experience any discomfort when you resume running, such as plantar fasciitis, stop your walk/run program immediately
- Cross train until you are free of pain and can start a walk-run program
- Cross training not only keeps you in shape while your injury heals, it also buys you time— time to seek out several medical opinions as to when you can safely return to running

—Olympian Lynn Kanuka

Q: *I suffer from arthritis, is it okay for me to run?*

A: It depends on the site of the arthritis. Improve your strength if it involves the hip, knees and/or ankles, then cycle, swim and, as the inflammation is controlled, try the walk/run program.

The 13-Week Program, Stretching & Strengthening Exercises

NOW IS THE TIME TO PUT TO WORK WHAT YOU'VE LEARNED about fitness and running. This chapter includes everything you will need: the 13-week walk/run program, some important stretching exercises for your warm-ups and cool-downs, some suggested strength training exercises to complement your running program and a training log. If you use these elements together and follow the precepts set out in this book, you are just weeks away from a new level of fitness.

The 13-week walk/run program is tried and proven. Refer back to Chapter 2 for information that will help you make the best use of it, including how to evaluate your fitness level, decide what to wear, determine where to run and set your training goals.

Proper warm-up, cool-down and stretching exercises are essential if you want to avoid injury. Those shown in this chapter are a key part of your training program. Chapter 3 also offers detailed information on how, when and how much you should be stretching, both before and after your training sessions.

Most successful athletes keep a training log, such as the one found in the *Beginning Runner's Journal,* the companion text to this book. Over time you will develop your own style of record keeping (see the general guidelines in Chapter 3), but meanwhile you can review Appendix A to see what yours might look like.

Good luck!

The 13-Week Walk/Run Program

Welcome to the 13-week walk/run program. This carefully tested exercise plan involves three training sessions each week, ranging in length from 27 to 61 minutes.

You'll notice that the program starts gradually, with lots of walking. A sports watch can help you time the walk/run segments of your sessions. If you find the pace too slow, bear with it and don't be tempted to skip ahead. You won't increase your fitness—just your risk of injury.

Finally, note that the times shown do not include your 5-minute warm-up and 5-minute cool-down in each training session. Be sure to allow extra time in your schedule for these essential components of your training.

WEEK 1

Session 1 (36 minutes)
Run 1 minute. Walk 2 minutes. Do this 12 times.

Session 2 (27 minutes)
Run 1 minute. Walk 2 minutes. Do this 9 times.

Session 3 (33 minutes)
Run 1 minute. Walk 2 minutes. Do this 11 times.

WEEK 2

Session 1 (44 minutes)
Run 2 minutes. Walk 2 minutes. Do this 11 times.

Session 2 (30 minutes)
Run 1 minute. Walk 2 minutes. Do this 10 times.

Session 3 (40 minutes)
Run 2 minutes. Walk 2 minutes. Do this 10 times.

WEEK 3

Session 1 (50 minutes)
Run 3 minutes. Walk 2 minutes. Do this 10 times.

Session 2 (36 minutes)
Run 2 minutes. Walk 2 minutes. Do this 9 times.

Session 3 (45 minutes)
Run 3 minutes. Walk 2 minutes. Do this 9 times.

WEEK 4 (Easy Recovery Week)

Session 1 (40 minutes)
Run 3 minutes. Walk 2 minutes. Do this 8 times.

Session 2 (28 minutes)
Run 2 minutes. Walk 2 minutes. Do this 7 times.

Session 3 (35 minutes)
Run 2 minutes. Walk 3 minutes. Do this 7 times.

WEEK 5

Session 1 (40 minutes)
Run 3 minutes. Walk 1 minute. Do this 10 times.

Session 2 (30 minutes)
Run 2 minutes. Walk 1 minute. Do this 10 times.

Session 3 (36 minutes)
Run 3 minutes. Walk 1 minute. Do this 9 times.

WEEK 6

Session 1 (48 minutes)
Run 5 minutes. Walk 1 minute. Do this 8 times.

Session 2 (36 minutes)
Run 2 minutes. Walk 1 minute. Do this 12 times.

Session 3 (40 minutes)
Run 3 minutes. Walk 1 minute. Do this 10 times.

WEEK 7

Session 1 (55 minutes)
Run 10 minutes. Walk 1 minute. Do this 5 times.

Session 2 (40 minutes)
Run 3 minutes. Walk 1 minute. Do this 10 times.

Session 3 (48 minutes)
Run 5 minutes. Walk 1 minute. Do this 8 times.

WEEK 8 (Easy Recovery Week)

Session 1 (44 minutes)
Run 10 minutes. Walk 1 minute. Do this 4 times.

Session 2 (32 minutes)
Run 3 minutes. Walk 1 minute. Do this 8 times.

Session 3 (42 minutes)
Run 5 minutes. Walk 1 minute. Do this 7 times.

WEEK 9

Session 1 (58 minutes)
Run 10 minutes. Walk 1 minute. Run 20 minutes. Walk 1 minute. Run 15 minutes.
Walk 1 minute. Run 10 minutes.

Session 2 (44 minutes)
Run 10 minutes. Walk 1 minute. Do this 4 times.

Session 3 (48 minutes)
Run 15 minutes. Walk 1 minute. Do this 3 times.

Note that as the run portions of the workout start to get longer, you will work toward running more continuously. Remember, you should be running at a comfortable talking pace, meaning you can carry on a conversation.

WEEK 10

Session 1 (61 minutes)
Run 30 minutes. Walk 1 minute. Run 30 minutes.

Session 2 (44 minutes)
Run 10 minutes. Walk 1 minute. Do this 4 times.

Session 3 (47 minutes)
Run 20 minutes. Walk 1 minute. Run 15 minutes. Walk 1 minute. Run 10 minutes.

WEEK 11

Session 1 (61 minutes)
Run 40 minutes. Walk 1 minute. Run 20 minutes.

Session 2 (44 minutes)
Run 10 minutes. Walk 1 minute. Do this 4 times.

Session 3 (47 minutes)
Run 20 minutes. Walk 1 minute. Run 15 minutes. Walk 1 minute. Run 10 minutes.

WEEK 12 (Easy Week)

Session 1 (50 minutes)
Run 50 minutes.

Session 2 (33 minutes)
Run 10 minutes. Walk 1 minute. Do this 3 times.

Session 3 (42 minutes)
Run 15 minutes. Walk 1 minute. Run 15 minutes. Walk 1 minute. Run 10 minutes.

WEEK 13

Session 1 (40 minutes)
Run 40 minutes.

Session 2 (33 minutes)
Run 10 minutes. Walk 1 minute. Do this 3 times.

Session 3
Event: See you at the finish line!

Stretching Exercises

Here are some stretches for the major muscle groups used in running and walking. Use these stretches as a guide to building your own routine. It's a good idea to work systematically from the calves up to the shoulders (or vice versa).

Before stretching, always start with 5 to 10 minutes of jogging on the spot or slow and easy running to warm your muscles. Then move into your pre-training stretching exercises. Hold each position (no bouncing) for approximately 10 seconds.

Your stretching routine should take no more than 3 to 5 minutes.

After your workout, use these same stretches to cool down. If you wish to work on increasing your flexibility, hold the stretches longer—anywhere from 15 seconds to 3 minutes—and repeat each stretch 2 to 3 times. Pay particular attention to the areas that you feel are the tightest; in runners these are usually the low back, hamstrings and calves.

Calf

1. Stand facing a wall, an arm's length plus 6 in (15 cm) away.
2. Place your right foot forward, halfway to the wall, and bend your right knee while keeping your left leg straight.
3. Lean into the wall, using your forearms for support and letting your left heel lift off the floor while keeping your head, neck, spine, pelvis and left leg in a straight line.
4. Exhale and shift your weight toward the wall while you attempt to press your left heel to the ground and your right knee toward the wall.
5. Hold the stretch and relax.
6. Repeat starting with your left leg forward.

Hamstring

This exercise requires a doorway.

1. Lie flat on your back, through a doorway, positioning your hips slightly in front of the doorframe, with the inside of your lower right thigh against one side of the doorframe.
2. Keeping your right leg straight and flat on the floor, exhale and raise your left leg up until your heel rests against the doorframe. Do not bend your left knee.
3. Hold the stretch and relax.
4. To increase the stretch, slide your buttocks closer to the doorframe, or lift the leg away from the doorframe to create a right angle.
5. Repeat with your right leg raised.

Iliotibial Band

1. Stand with your left side towards a wall, an arm's length away, feet together.
2. Extend your left arm sideways at shoulder height so the flat of your hand is against the wall and you are leaning toward it.
3. Place your right hand on the side of your right hip.
4. Exhale, keeping your legs straight, tightening your buttocks, and pushing your left hip in toward the wall until you feel the stretch down the outside of your left leg.
5. Hold the stretch and relax.
6. Repeat on the right side.

Quadriceps

Avoid this exercise if it causes pain in your knee joint.

1. Stand facing a wall, an arm's length away. Place your right hand against the wall for balance and support.
2. Bend your left leg at the knee and raise the foot behind you until you can grasp it with your left hand.
3. Slightly bend your right leg at the knee and be sure to keep your lower back straight.
4. Pull your left heel toward your buttock.
5. Hold the stretch and relax.
6. Repeat with your right leg.

Groin

1. Sit upright on the floor, with your back against a wall.
2. Bend your knees up then let them fall to the sides with the soles of your feet facing each other.
3. Grasp your ankles with both hands and pull your heels toward your buttocks.
4. Rest your elbows on the inside of your thighs.
5. Slowly push your knees toward the floor until you feel the stretch in your groin.
6. Hold the stretch and relax.

Hip Flexor

(For those who are unable to kneel, this exercise can be done while sitting on the edge of a chair, and assuming the same position as illustrated but without the knee touching the ground.)

1. Stand with your feet together, then take one stride forward with your right foot.
2. Flexing your right knee, slowly lower your body toward the ground, finishing with your left knee touching the floor and your right heel flat on the floor.
3. Rest your hands just above the right knee and keep that knee bent at no more than a right angle.
4. For some, getting into this position will be enough. If you wish to increase the stretch, exhale while pushing your left hip forward and increasing the stretch on the left side.
5. Hold the stretch and relax.
6. Repeat with your left foot forward.

Gluteal

1. Lie flat on your back with your legs straight and arms out to the sides.
2. Bend the left knee and raise it toward your chest, grasping your leg under the knee or thigh with your right hand.
3. Keep your head, shoulders and elbows flat on the floor.
4. Exhale as you pull your knee across your body toward the floor.
5. Hold the stretch and relax.
6. Repeat with the right leg.

Lower Back

1. Lie flat on your back with your knees bent to form a right angle and your arms out to the sides.
2. Exhale, and slowly lower both knees to the left side.
3. Keep your elbows, head and shoulders flat on the floor.
4. Hold the stretch and relax.
5. Repeat on the left side.

Lower Back

1. Lie flat on your back with your legs straight out.
2. Bend your knees and slide your heels toward your buttocks.
3. Using both hands, grasp behind your knees. (It's not important to keep your knees together—they should be comfortable.)
4. Exhale, pulling your knees toward your chest and slowly lifting your hips from the floor, while keeping your head and shoulders on the floor.
5. Hold the stretch and relax.

Shoulder

1. Sit with your right arm raised in front of you at shoulder height.
2. Bring your right hand across your chest and place it on the back of your left shoulder, keeping your elbow at shoulder height.
3. Grasp your right elbow with your left hand.
4. Exhale and pull your elbow in toward your left shoulder.
5. Hold the stretch and relax.
6. Repeat with your left arm.

Strength Training Exercises

Strength trianing is beneficial for runners of all ages—at any level of performance. Here are some sample exercises for starting a strength-training program.

Before starting a new routine, consult a fitness professional experienced in designing these programs. Aim for two or three strength-training sessions per week.

Start your workout with a proper warm-up: some low-intensity aerobic activity such as stationary cycling, walking or light jogging, followed by some light stretching. Then, begin working with lighter weights. How light? Consult a professional to find out what's right for you. If you don't have anyone to ask, make sure you can lift the weight with little effort for at least 10 repetitions. Err on the side of caution.

As a general guideline, start by doing one or two sets of 10 to 15 repetitions for each exercise—do the minimum number of repetitions in the beginning, and build your way up to the maximum. As you become more confident and competent, gradually increase the weight or resistance.

Lower Body

Lunges

1. Stand tall with your hands on your hips and your feet shoulder-width apart.
2. Keep your back straight and your head up.
3. Step forward slowly with your left leg. Bend your left knee and lower your body forward and down so that your weight is over this knee. Make sure that your kneecap does not extend past your toes. Keep your back leg relaxed and slightly bent so that your knee almost touches the floor. Your trunk should remain upright. Step backward to the start position.
4. Exhale as you step forward, and inhale as you return to the start position.
5. Repeat this exercise with your right leg.

Step-Ups

1. Stand tall with feet shoulder-width apart.
2. Keep back straight (flat) and your head upright, eyes looking forward.
3. Step up with your right leg on a bench, box or other stable platform.
4. The height of the platform will depend on your strength and level of fitness. The maximum height of your platform should not exceed the level required to place your femur (thigh bone) in a horizontal position.
5. Once your right foot is firmly on the platform, shift your hips forward and step up on the platform using only your right leg, until you are in a fully erect posture.
6. Follow through with the trailing leg.
7. Step down, first with the right leg, then with the left leg.

8. Repeat the sequence 10 times with a right-leg lead and followed 10 times with a left-leg lead.
9. Remember to exhale as you step up and inhale as you step down.

Squats

1. Stand tall with your feet shoulder-width apart.
2. Keeping your back flat, move your hips back and down slowly until your thigh bone (femur) is horizontal.
3. In the squat position, your knees should not line up ahead of your toes and your head should be in a neutral position with your eyes looking forward.
4. Slowly return to a standing position and then repeat the sequence.
5. Exhale as you ascend and inhale as you descend.

Abdominals

Abdominal Crunches

1. Lie face up on the floor with your lower legs resting on an exercise ball (or a chair).
2. Position your body so that your thighs are at a 90–degree angle.

3. Folding your arms across your chest, curl your body toward your thighs until your upper back is off the floor. Slowly return to the start position. Be careful not to bounce or jerk your body.
4. Exhale as you curl up, and inhale as you return to the start position.

Upper Body

Shoulder Press

1. Sit tall in a chair with your feet in front of your knees. Be sure that your back does not touch the back of the chair.
2. Keep your back straight and your head up.
3. Sit on the middle of the band and hold one end of the elastic in each hand.
4. Push both hands overhead simultaneously to a fully extended position.
5. Return hands to shoulder height, making a V-position with the band.
6. Hands should maintain a palms forward position throughout the movement.
7. Repeat sequence 10 times.
8. Exhale through the push phase, and inhale as you return your hands to the shoulder position.
9. You can adjust the resistance by lengthening or shortening the elastic.

Lat Pulldown

1. Sit tall in a chair with your feet in front of your knees and your back not touching the back of the chair.
2. Keep your back straight with your head up and eyes forward.
3. Hold the ends of the elastic, one in each hand with the middle of the band looped over an overhead object (e.g., a coat hook).
4. In a start position with the arms extended and hands overhead, palms facing forward, pull downward until hands reach a shoulder position.
5. Release slowly, allowing elastic to pull hands back into an overhead position.
6. Repeat sequence 10 times.

7. Exhale through the push phase, and inhale as you return your hands to the shoulder position.
8. You can adjust the resistance by lengthening or shortening the elastic.

Chest Press

1. Sit tall in a chair with your feet in front of your knees and your back not touching the back of the chair.
2. Keep your back straight, your head up and eyes forward.
3. Hold the ends of the elastic, one in each hand, with the middle of the band looped behind your back.
4. With your hands at chest level in a palms forward position, press forward (horizontally) to an arms fully extended position.
5. Release slowly, allowing the elastic to return hands to the chest level.
6. Repeat sequence 10 times.
7. Exhale through the push phase, and inhale as you return your hands to the shoulder position.
8. You can adjust the resistance by lengthening or shortening the elastic.

Seated Row

1. Sit tall in a chair with your feet in front of your knees and your back not touching the back of the chair.
2. Keep your back straight, your head up and eyes forward.
3. Hold the ends of the elastic, one in each hand, with the middle of the band looped around an object directly in front of you (e.g., a door knob, table leg).
4. Begin with arms extended horizontally and palms facing the floor.
5. Pull hands back to a mid-chest position.
6. Release slowly, allowing the elastic to return arms to a fully extended and horizontal position.
7. Repeat sequence 10 times.
8. Exhale through the push phase, and inhale as you return your hands to the shoulder position.
9. You can adjust the resistance by lengthening or shortening the elastic.

What's Next?

WHEN YOU HAVE COMPLETED THE 13-WEEK WALK/RUN program, you will likely think of yourself as a different person. You will have taken yourself to a new level of fitness, and probably given your self-confidence a boost as well. You will know that if you set your mind to something, you can achieve it. If you have trained with others, you will doubtless have made new friends outside your traditional circle. But when the program is over, you may find yourself asking, "Now what?"

From a physiological standpoint, your successful completion of the program brings you both good news and bad. The good news is that the cardiovascular (heart and lung) fitness you have worked so patiently to develop over the past 13 weeks is relatively easy to maintain. All you have to do is carry on doing what you have been doing—exercising aerobically three times a week for 30 to 40 minutes. You do not have to perpetually push yourself further. If, however, you want to continue to improve your fitness level, you're going to have to continue challenging your body. One way to do this is to follow the 13-week run faster program found in Appendix C of this book (see page 197). You will notice that it offers additional challenges, including hill repeat sessions and interval training. But remember: do not begin the intermediate program until you have completed the 13-week walk/run program and, even then, only if you are running regularly. Otherwise you will risk getting injured.

The bad news is that if you've thought of completing the program as the end of the road, the fitness you have worked so hard to attain will slowly seep away, like water into sand. By the end of a month, it will be vastly diminished. You may find it unfair that you worked so hard and

Barb

Barb, 41, wasn't diagnosed with postpartum depression until some time after the birth of her second child. At that point both her doctor and her psychiatrist strongly recommended that she get more exercise. Barb had avoided any kind of physically strenuous sport for the better part of a decade. "For me it was like starting from scratch, so I did the walking program [see Appendix B, page 193] and that got me going."

Quite quickly she found her training sessions becoming an important part of her life. "I realized that what I'd really needed was some time for myself. My family came to understand that I was a lot happier if I had that time. You know how it is—if mom's happy, everybody's happy." The social contacts she made throughout the program gave her a valuable outlet as well. "The people I've met have been great; everybody's been really supportive."

Like a lot of people who start with the walking program, Barb is considering moving on and doing the 13-week walk/run program, but she's in no hurry. Armed with her new-found confidence in her abilities, she's discovered mountain biking and has already worked her way up to the intermediate trails in the hills where she lives. "The walking program showed me the benefits of exercise and it just sort of propelled me into mountain biking," she says happily.

Squeezed between the pressures of family and her full-time job at a local community college, Barb learned that to be all things to so many people, she also had to be true to herself. Her fitness program gives her both the time and the space she needs to cope with the stresses of day-to-day living.

then don't get to rest on your laurels for a while, but that's the way it is. Your body will return to the state it was in before you started the program.

Some people don't mind. They may have taken on the program simply to see if they could do it or because friends challenged them. Sometimes these people drift away from fitness altogether and never come back. It's a personal choice—though not a very healthy one.

Other people find that when they get to the end of the program and don't have a schedule to follow, their motivation slips out the door. It's not so much a choice: they're just lost without a script, and before they realize it, they're out of shape again.

If this happens to you, or if a life event—a sickness in the family, say, or a crisis at work—prevents you from maintaining your current level of fitness, you can always start over again. It isn't as bad as it sounds. You already know that in your hands you have both the prescription and the cure. You can simply go back to the beginning, start over, and in 13 weeks you'll be back on top. Nor will you be alone. Many people who let their fitness slide after completing the program eventually become unhappy about huffing and puffing like an old steam locomotive every time they have to sprint for the bus, and return to the program several or even many months later. It is infinitely better to start again than it is to quit for good.

On the other hand, by following the program, most of you will have found that you actually enjoy your new level of fitness and would like to do whatever is necessary to maintain it. To begin, taking a few days off after you complete the program isn't going to hurt your fitness level at

A 1997 study by researchers at Stanford University showed that people who exercise, maintain a healthy weight and don't smoke are only half as likely to become disabled by age 75 as people who don't have these habits.

all. Quite the opposite, in fact; your body will probably be grateful for the opportunity to recover, especially if you were training for a running event and your program culminated in a 10-k run. As the week following the race or program completion goes by, however, you should start thinking about how you are going to follow up and get into a regular program of maintenance.

There are a number of ways to stay in top form. You can simply continue with your current time commitment of three 30- to 40-minute sessions a week, which should be relatively easy because your body is already programmed to do it. If you find the longer sessions too onerous or time consuming, you can stick to half-hour sessions during the week, provided you make time for at least one session of 45 to 60 minutes on the weekend. You can adjust the time you spend training to suit your schedule; just keep in mind that the key to maintaining fitness is frequency and intensity—and that it is a lot less work to maintain a fitness level than to establish one; working out for even 20 minutes is better than nothing. Or you can train by engaging in 10- to 15-minute "spurts" of exercise throughout the day. If you don't feel like running at all, a fast walk will suffice to get your heart rate up and help you maintain a healthy level of fitness.

If you find your motivation slipping away, sign up for one of the many running and walking events in your community. There are runners everywhere these days, and most of them love getting together. The events they attend are partly a way to gauge progress and partly a way to socialize. Your local running-shoe store or community center will likely have a schedule of such events. As well, walking clubs abound and their weekly activities are often listed in local newspapers.

If you complete the program and decide that running isn't for you, don't despair. Running isn't for everyone, which is probably a good thing, because if it were, some running paths would get very crowded. Still, not loving to run shouldn't mean retreating back to the sofa and the remote control. As discussed in Chapter 6, there are all kinds of other enjoyable aerobic activities. Cycling, swimming, cross-country skiing and hiking are excellent alternatives to running, as are in-line skating, kayaking, aerobics to music, walking or even just putting in some time on the stair climber at your local gym.

The important thing is that you find an aerobic activity you enjoy. The more you enjoy it, the more likely you are to find the time for it. Futhermore, although you need to keep some kind of aerobic activity at the center of your fitness plan, you might like to sample some anaerobic, stop-and-go sports as well. If you enjoy games, you might try soccer, squash, softball, volleyball, tennis, basketball, hockey or badminton. Some of these activities may look as though they involve a lot of standing around, but keep in mind that you'll get as much out of them as you're prepared to invest. Badminton can be a leisurely activity, or you can work hard and break a real sweat—it's up to you. The important thing is to get and stay fit by doing activities you enjoy.

When approaching any sport, remember the three rules of exercise—moderation, consistency and rest—and don't expect to be an expert right away. Each sport requires unique skills and it will take you a while to

When the 13 weeks are over

- Continue exercising three times a week
- Join a running or walking club
- Sign up for running or walking events—check your local running-shoe store or community center
- Continue to keep an exercise/activity log to record your workouts
- Try other activities—cycling, swimming and hiking are just a few of the numerous, excellent alternatives

acquire them. Each time you take up a new activity, you'll find there are as many comfort-zone barriers to cross as you are willing to take on. As well, you will invariably reach plateaus of competence that only patience and practice will take you beyond. If you're having trouble progressing, take lessons. Or, seek assistance from a more experienced participant: every sport has a dedicated core of enthusiasts who are glad to help out newcomers and show them the ropes.

In addition to taking part in aerobic and anaerobic activities, it's a good idea to do some strength training. This can involve weights or circuit training. If you want to increase your strength and also push some comfort-zone barriers, try climbing.

No matter which activities you choose, it's essential to prepare yourself properly. This includes warming up and

Lisa

Lisa, then 32, wasn't sure she would run forever. After three years of it, she was in the best shape of her life, but she heard the siren of other activities calling her name. "My boyfriend's a climber and he took me out to this mountain," she says. "The only really technical part was the last 10 feet (3 meters) and he told me I didn't have to do it if I didn't want to. When we got near the top, he and his friends scrambled up to the highest point.

"There was no pressure or anything but I wanted to be there too, so I crawled up the last bit of rock almost to the top—but I wasn't prepared for what I found when I got there: the rock face just fell away on the other side. I froze. My boyfriend helped guide me down to a ledge and I sat there drinking water and waiting for the panic to subside. He told me it didn't matter that I'd only managed to get near the top and not actually touch it; it counted either way. I listened to him say this but I knew it wasn't true; I knew I'd have to try again.

"It was easier the next time, partly because I knew what to expect. I crawled up and put my hand on the highest point and then scrambled back down. I think it was the hardest thing I've ever done. "I still like running," she swears, "but there are a lot of mountains to climb out there."

cooling down, eating nutritious food, wearing suitable clothing and equipment, and staying aware of the potential for injuries. In other words, the basics you learned in this book are relevant to all the activities you may take up.

Deciding on Your Next Challenge

Regardless of whether you want to maintain your current fitness level, diversify your exercise program or improve your 10-k time, the important point to remember is that you are already a fitness success. By now, you understand that setting a goal and having a clear plan of how to get there are the keys to success.

Many of you may already have your next fitness goal in mind, but for those who don't, you may want to consider some of the following questions to assist you in establishing your next athletic milestone:

- How long have you been maintaining a regular running routine?
- How much time do you have to commit to your exercise program?
- Have you been injury free for the duration of your 13-week walk/run program?
- Have you enjoyed your running program enough to continue or increase the distance or intensity?
- Do you feel mentally and physically ready for another fitness challenge?
- Are you bored with running? Do you feel the need to try another athletic activity?

Training to Run Faster

If you have maintained a regular running schedule for at least a year, have been free of injury for several weeks and

Making the transition

What is the biggest difference between training to run a 10-k race versus a half or full marathon?

- The time commitment and family support needed are greater
- You will be training for significantly longer periods of time
- There will be a "tired" factor that takes its toll; you will probably need to be in bed earlier, and will have less energy for other physical activities and less free time

Note: Before embarking on a more demanding running program, check with your medical practitioner to ensure you are heart-healthy and have no running-related aches and pains

—*Olympian Lynn Kanuka*

want to increase the intensity of your training, you may be ready to embark on the new challenge of running faster. The goal of an improved 10-k race time is exciting, and quite different from the sole objective of completing a 10-k event. Essential to achieving the goal of an improved race time is a diverse and well-organized training program.

Employing a variety of training techniques will both improve your fitness and help you maintain motivation. Interval training, tempo running, hill and fartlek training are the four general running workouts used by successful runners to build strength and improve speed. Most running experts suggest a weekly schedule that includes one or more speed and strength workouts. If you're a beginning runner, try incorporating one speed workout a week into your running program for the first six to eight weeks. If you already run three times a week, make one of those runs a speed-training session.

RUNNER PROFILE

Suzanne

Suzanne is a full-time teacher who has been running a few times a week for almost four years. The 27-year-old recently completed the 13-week run faster program. "During the school year I'm pretty busy with my students, plus I try to coach the girl's basketball and cross-country running teams. But when I run regularly I cope with stress more easily. It just makes me feel good.

"I had been looking for a new running challenge, and the Run Faster program was great. I wanted to improve my 10-k time and run one in under 60 minutes. But I did more than that. I completed the *Vancouver Sun* Run™ in 52 minutes!"

While Suzanne is not able to commit more time to her training program than 3–4 times a week, she does feel that she has the running bug. "My next running goal is to introduce regular speed training into one of my weekly runs. I've learned some great ways to improve my speed, such as hill repeats and tempo workouts, which are challenging and fun. And I now have a friend at work who has agreed to join me for one or two runs a week. With some good planning, I think I might be able to beat my 52-minute *Sun* Run™ time."

Once you have completed approximately eight consecutive speed-training workouts over the course of eight weeks, and if you are not injured, you may want to introduce a second speed session into your weekly running schedule. The second session, or speed workout, should be different from the first session. For example, if your first eight weeks of speed training included one hill-training session a week, the next session you incorporate might be a fartlek or interval workout.

Like your 13-week walk/run program, consistency is necessary to improve speed. Given that determination can wane for even the most focused individuals, finding a training partner with similar goals is a good way to improve your motivation and the likelihood of staying on track. If fitness levels vary, speed training can be easily modified to accommodate even the most diverse training groups. By doing shorter speed intervals and regrouping during your rest breaks, groups are able to provide each other with the support and motivation needed to complete demanding workouts.

Hill training

Running up hills builds muscle and cardiovascular endurance, and makes a good transition to speed work. Hills also add challenge to more advanced workouts. And hill training is easy to adapt to groups of runners with varying speeds and endurance levels. Remember, you need to treat each hill-training segment as an individual workout and recover before repeating it.

When running up a hill, try not to lean forward; focus on keeping your balance, shortening your leg stride, lifting your knees a little higher and keeping those arms pumping. Before you know it, you will be going down the other side. Use gravity as much as possible and lengthen your stride to keep your hips over your feet.

In planning your hill training session, choose a hill that is at least 110 yards (100 meters) long and not too steep. You want a hill with a gentle incline that you can run up, not one that's too steep. Your hill repeats can be based on time or distance, it's up to you. For example: run hard up the hill for 45 seconds, stop and regroup with your training partners, then jog back down to the start of the hill at an easy pace that allows you to catch your breath. Repeat 5 to 7 times, depending on your fitness level. A word of caution: if you haven't caught your breath by the time you reach the bottom of the hill, you are pushing yourself too hard. It's a good idea to use this as a gauge for how hard you are working. You want to push yourself, but you also want to live to run another day. After about eight weeks, gradually increase your number of hill segments.

Regardless of the type of speed session, always make sure you start your run with at least a 10-minute warm-up at an easy pace. After completing the speed session, it's also a good idea to do a 10-minute cool-down at an easy pace. By including an easy pace before and after a speed session you are able to warm up and loosen your muscles.

If there aren't any hills in your neighborhood, there are alternatives to building strength and endurance. A few suggestions:

- Treadmill workouts, where you elevate the machine to a 7 per cent grade, are a great way to simulate hill running. Depending on the machine, you can do pre-programmed workouts or manually adjust the speed so that your workouts mirror those done on land, as outlined above.

- Bike or step machine intervals are great workouts. Warm up for 10 minutes, increase the intensity for 4 or 5 minutes, then recover. After a few sessions, try adding a second repeat to the workout.

- Bleacher steps at your neighborhood baseball field are a challenging and fun way to build leg strength. Warm up, run up the steps at a difficult pace, then walk back down—consider this one set. Gradually increase the number of sets as your strength improves. Remember, if you are still out of breath at the bottom of the stairs you're pushing yourself too hard.

Interval training

This type of training is a combination of running at a faster than normal pace and walking during the recovery stage. The goal is to increase your capacity to carry oxygen through your system and improve your muscle endurance. You will be running at a slightly higher speed for a short period, followed by a recovery period in which you will walk or jog slowly. You can measure your intervals by time or distance; it's up to you.

Remember to begin each speed-training session with a 10-minute warm-up and end each session with a 10-minute cool-down, followed by some easy stretches. Warm-up and cool-down running is done at an easy speed that allows your muscles to prepare for and recover from the intensity of speed training.

If speed training is new for you, you may want to start with 2 minutes at your goal race pace, followed by 2 minutes easy. The 2 minutes easy is your recovery period where you can walk or jog easy. The 2 minutes of hard running followed by 2 minutes of easy running or walking makes up one set. Try three sets for the first three weeks before gradually introducing a fourth and fifth set. For beginners or those new to speed work, don't attempt any more than five sets for the first six to eight months of speed training.

Deciding the distance or time of each workout is up to you. Some runners may want to stick with the same workout for a few months, but for others this approach may become boring. Usually it's a good idea to vary your workouts to keep things interesting and help maintain motivation. Other interval workouts for beginners include:

- 5 minutes hard with $2\frac{1}{2}$ minutes easy. Repeat 3 times, gradually building to 5 sets
  OR
- 3 1-k repeats with a rest period that is approximately half of the acceleration time

Remember, the goal of your rest period is to recover from the hard session so that your breathing can return almost to normal. If you are unable to catch your breath between intervals you are pushing yourself too hard. If this is the case, ease off a little during the intense periods. It takes time to understand how hard to push yourself. Also, how you feel can vary from one run to the next. Outside factors such as wind, rain, heat—as well as stress and sleep—play a role in how hard and fast you can run on a given day. It's always better to start easy so that you can push yourself at the end. By going out too hard, you could end the interval or session feeling like you cannot run another step.

Fartlek training

Fartleks are a series of random bursts done during a continuous walk or run. These bursts can range anywhere from 20 seconds to 3 minutes and are performed every 2 to 4 minutes. Their duration and speed is up to you. But the emphasis should be on running for significant periods at a pace faster than your normal training and racing paces. Each hard effort is followed by a recovery stage, when the pace is reduced to a point where breathing and pulse rate return to near normal resting rate. Still, the key is to keep moving. This type of workout is well suited for trail running over varied terrain.

Before starting your fartlek session, remember to warm up for 10 minutes and to include a 10-minute cooldown upon completing the speed session. Beginners can start with 1 minute hard followed by 1 minute easy. Try this 10 times to start with. After six weeks, gradually build up to 12 and then 15 repeats. Another suggestion is to use landmarks such as telephone poles as indicators for speeding up and slowing down. For example: run hard for two telephone poles, then easy for two poles. Repeat 7 times and gradually increase to 15 repeats.

Tempo training

Tempo running is when you maintain a continuous pace that is faster than your easy run, but one you can maintain for up to an hour if it were a race. Tempo runs teach the

**Taking
a break**

It is important to build a
holiday into your program:

- Choose to be active,
  but not scheduled
- Plan *at least* two weeks
  in the year when you
  do *not* exercise—so that
  when you start back,
  you'll feel newly
  motivated
- Plan a "destination"
  race and holiday there
  after the event. You will
  feel like you've earned
  the right to kick back
  and relax

—*Olympian Lynn Kanuka*

body to run faster before fatiguing, and, like the other speed sessions described in this section, can be done based on time or distance. Beginners might want to start a tempo run that is about 2 miles long (just over 3 kilometers), or 15 to 18 minutes in length. After six weeks of successful training, add 3/4 mile (about 1 kilometer), or 7 minutes every couple of weeks until you reach 3 3/4 miles (6 kilometers), or 25 minutes. Remember to include your 10-minute warm-up and cool-down before and after every tempo training session. Stretching should also be done for about 10 to 15 minutes at the end of each run.

Training to Run Farther

If you have completed the 13-week walk/run program and you continue to enjoy running and want to increase the duration of your runs, you may be interested in the training schedules and running regimens of half- and full-marathon runners. Those who embark on an 18-week marathon or 15-week half-marathon training schedule have, for the most part, run consistently for at least six months. The majority run 45 minutes 3 to 4 times a week as well as one longer run of $1\frac{1}{2}$ to 2 hours, depending on the goal distance.

If running farther is your new goal, as with your previous walk/run program you will have three training sessions each week for the first few months. Like before, most training sessions will take about an hour to complete.

To start your run farther program, turn to the next chapter, Is Running a Marathon for You?, to learn more about training to run farther.

The Race Is On

Numerous people who complete the 13-week walk/run program probably knew even before they started that running was the sport for them. Some will use running as a release and always do it alone. Others will think of it as an important adjunct to their social life—a way to make new friends no matter where they go. Many of these people will join running groups and in a few years will be talking about the "thousands" of miles they have run and the dozens of events they have entered. Still others will want above all to race.

There are a number of good reasons for entering races, but the main one should always be because they are fun. There's a great sense of camaraderie around these events and some runners go just because they love to meet up with the kinds of people who participate in them. Some high-profile races include the *Vancouver Sun* Run™ in British Columbia; the Great North Run in Newcastle, England; Around the Bays in Auckland, New Zealand; the Sydney City to Surf in Australia; the Bloomsday 12-k in Spokane, Washington; the Peachtree Classic in Atlanta, Georgia, and the Bay to Breakers in San Francisco—but there are a host of others. These events attract beginning runners and people who have been doing it for years. Few of the participants will care much what your time is; they are interested only in their own—and in having fun.

Such events can also be educational. Races are often preceded by running clinics at which expert runners, doctors and physiologists host forums on various running-

 Among cancer survivors who responded to a 1997 University of Utah nursing survey, 90 per cent said exercise made them feel more relaxed and refreshed, and 94 per cent said it made them feel better about their overall health.

related topics. What's more, running-equipment manufacturers often set up booths to promote their products, so that the events also serve as miniature trade fairs and conferences.

Although only one person can cross the finish line first, there's a general consensus that anyone who competes in a race wins simply by taking part. What's more, many races now have separate categories that allow entrants to test their mettle against people their own age. For example, you could come in 62nd or 178th overall, but still wind up 5th in the 45- to 50-year-old group. Still, you don't have to get caught up in competing—just enjoy yourself.

You might also want to experiment with different distances. There are lots of 5-k and 10-k "fun runs." If you find you enjoy participating in them, you can move on to the building up to the half-marathon training program included in this book and perhaps enter longer-distance events. But try to be sure long-distance running is what you really want before subjecting yourself to the rigors associated with it. Marathon running is not for everybody any more than every climber needs to scale Mount Everest. If you get into a race that's over your head and halfway through have to pull over with nausea and cramps, you're not likely to want to come back. You'll also be exposing yourself to the possibility of injury. The best strategy is to pick a race that's well within your comfort zone and give yourself a chance to complete it.

Providing motivation is one of the biggest reasons to enter a race—maybe the best one. Having a race date set on your calendar can get you to lace up your runners and go even when your heart says to unlace and sit. Having told all your friends you're going to do it, you won't want everyone asking you how you did and then have to explain that you "didn't feel like it." In racing, success also breeds success. If you do well, you'll be further motivated to train harder and do even better the next time.

If you've been cross training, you may want to think about competing in duathlons or triathlons. As their names imply, these events include more than one sport. Duathlons usually consist of running and cycling. In triathlons, you get to start with a bracing swim, then cycle, then run. The length of these events, like those of running events, vary considerably. A short-course duathlon can feature a 5-k run followed by a 20-k bike ride, capped off with another 5-k run. On the other hand, an "ironman" triathlon can include a 2.4-mile (4-k) swim, a 112-mile (180-k) bike ride and then a full marathon (26.2 miles/ 42 k). They don't call it "ironman" for nothing!

Ready to Race

Bruce Angus, 35, a self-professed "amateur professional" who has been entering events on and off for the better part of 20 years, discovered running as a young man in high school. He grew to love the sport and reckons he has been in as many as 100 events, finishing as high as 13th overall in an ironman triathlon with a time of 10 hours and 41 minutes. After years of trial and error, of good finishes and bad, he's learned a lot about event preparation. "The first thing you want to do is make sure you've done all your training before race day," he says with a chuckle. (Don't laugh. You'd be surprised how many people think they can train half-heartedly—or even enthusiastically— for a week or two before a race and then go the distance.)

✓ Running two to three times a week can reduce your risk of gallstone disease by 20 to 40 per cent, according to a 1997 study by the Harvard School of Public Health at Harvard Medical School.

Before competing, Angus is like a race-car driver: he likes to scope out the track and get a feel for the environment he's going to be running in. "I like to drive, cycle or even run the track before the race. I find it's not very good if you go into a race not knowing how far it is. If you've been through the course, you have a clear understanding of the terrain and you can visualize moving through it, where you're going to pass people. It's also good to know what kind of surface it is, whether it's grass or gravel or pavement. The kind of surface and the distance will dictate what kind of footwear you're going to choose. I have three types of running shoes I can use, depending on the course. If I'm going to be running on trails, I'll want more support, but for any race over 10 k, I'll go with less support and more cushioning. If it's a sprint, say a 5-k fun run, I'll wear lightweight racing flats."

RUNNER PROFILE

Lynn

It took a move all the way across North America to get Lynn into running, but now that she's started she says she's never going to stop. "After I moved, I wanted to meet people who shared the same kinds of interests I did," says the 29-year-old dietitian. A competitive swimmer in her youth, Lynn not only wanted new friends, she wanted the friends to be fit and active people like herself. She heard about a running clinic and signed up.

"It's been a great experience and I've met such a variety of people. They're my friends now, so I don't know what I'd do if I didn't go running. We have a running club and we meet every Saturday. We've also gone to a play together and on some other social outings as well."

Because her main goal is fitness in general, Lynn supplements her running with other activities, such as swimming and in-line skating. "I'm aiming for a balance because it seems to be more in keeping with my lifestyle. There are also health reasons for doing other sports. As well, if I run all the time and don't do anything else, I get bored."

Although his more obsessive training days are behind him, Angus still runs three times a week, and then looks for time in his schedule to squeeze in both cycling and swimming. That may seem rather extreme, but he has his heart set on another ironman appearance.

Whatever your motivation for entering an event, a few moments' planning can make all the difference in your enjoyment of it. Here are some simple guidelines for pre-event preparation.

- Rest up the last few days before the event. Squeezing in more training at the last minute will not get you any fitter. Plan to get an optimal amount of sleep during the last 72 hours.
- Check the weather forecast the day before and plan accordingly. You need to consider what you will wear during the run as well as what you will wear after it.
- Pack your bag and pin your number on your shirt the night before. Items to consider (depending on the time of year): a complete change of clothes, extra shoes, a hat, gloves, toilet paper (you'd be surprised how often it's needed), petroleum jelly, a towel, a rain jacket and a bottle of water.
- Be sure to drink plenty of water—two to three glasses, one to two hours before the start. (Also, don't forget to drink water at the aid stations along the running route.)
- When driving to the race, give yourself plenty of time to park, visit the restroom and warm up.
- Warm up properly. Although there is no guarantee this will prevent injuries, a combination of light jogging

A sample weekly program for the active person

Monday 45-minute run (on a trail in the park)

Tuesday 25-minute swim (front crawl)

Wednesday 50-minute run (steady pace)

Thursday weight-training session (10 exercises, 3 sets each)

Friday 45-minute run (varying pace)

Saturday weight-training session (10 exercises, 3 sets each)

Sunday Rest

A 1997 study at Harvard University found that women who exercise produce a less potent form of estrogen than those who do not. The study concluded that women who exercise can halve their risk of developing breast and uterine cancer.

and easy stretching prior to the start will increase your heart rate and help loosen joints and muscles, preparing your body for the activity ahead.

• Try to keep as warm and dry as possible before the start of the race.

Whether you choose to enter events or not, and whether you wish to continue running or not, completing the 13-week walk/run program will have helped you increase your fitness level and gain a new appreciation for the virtues and joys of exercise. There's always more to learn about fitness in general and running in particular, and you can continue to expand your knowledge by reading, attending conferences and events, signing up for seminars, joining a running group or just chatting with friends who have similar interests. If you decide you want to run farther and faster, consider the 13-week training program at the intermediate level included in the appendices of this book.

Whatever you decide to do, try to make exercise a part of your life. You'll be happier and healthier because of it, and in the end, that's what makes it all worthwhile.

11

Is Running a
Marathon for You?

EVER THOUGHT OF RUNNING A HALF OR FULL MARATHON?
Did you enjoy the 13-week walk/run program and are now asking
yourself, "What next? Can I run farther than 10 k?" or "How else can
I improve my fitness?" If you are, you might consider training for a
half or full marathon. But before you jump into a more intense training program, there are a few things you need to know. In this chapter we discuss the fundamentals behind half and full marathons. We
have also compiled some commonly asked questions and answers,
training tips and a suggested training program to get you started.

The Marathon

The first thing you need to know is the definition of a marathon: it's
a race of 26.2 miles (42 kilometers). If you were to drive this distance
in your car, it would take you almost 30 minutes traveling at 60 mph.
But don't let that scare you. What you *do* need to think about is if this
is the right time for you to embark on this challenge. Although completing a marathon is no longer viewed as a Herculean endeavor but
the fitness goal for thousands of North Americans, both the 26.2-mile
full marathon and 13.1-mile (21-kilometer) half marathon are still

extraordinary goals. To complete either one is a remarkable achievement. Before you decide on whether attempting one of these races is for you, it's important to first understand the time, commitment and tremendous patience required to prepare for such events.

A brief history of the marathon

The marathon has a long and interesting history that dates back to a hot summer's day in 490 BC. This 2,500-year-old Greek legend is almost certainly fictionalized, with the soldier Pheilippides running from a battlefield near Marathon, Greece, to Athens, to deliver the news of a Greek victory over the Persians. According to the history books, Pheilippides then collapsed and died of exhaustion. But his historic run, even though it has the makings of a fable, inspired one of the world's greatest sporting events: the marathon, which would remain a relatively

RUNNER PROFILE

Sarah

Two years ago, Sarah quit smoking and started running with her friend, Bob. Now, after completing the 13-week walk/run program, the 30-year-old teacher has decided to train for her first full marathon. Last year she ran a half marathon. And while she found it difficult, she's proud of her achievement.

On race day next spring, Sarah says she'll rely on the inspiration of her late father who, two years ago, died of lung cancer. She will also run for her friend, Bob, who inspired her to take up running.

Sarah was never active in high school and college, preferring to spend her free time painting and reading. Other than quitting smoking, Sarah views her commitment to running a half marathon one of the most significant challenges she has ever faced. But she's confident that she will make it to the finish line. She is following her four-month marathon training program and, with the exception of one cold that derailed her for a few days, everything has gone according to plan. She feels fitter and healthier now than ever before.

obscure event for the next 2,000 years. It was not until the late 1970s to early '80s that fun runs became popular.

Today, women compete in road races of all distances. From the 5-k races to the marathon and ultra-marathon distances, female runners make up at least half of all participants. This was not always the case. It was long thought that women were not physiologically capable of handling endurance activities, and they were prohibited from participating in distances greater than 800 meters. In the late '60s and early '70s, however, the increasing interest in recreational running had a strong effect on competitive events. This, along with the women's liberation movement, resulted in women being allowed to compete in longer races. Finally in 1984, at the Los Angeles Olympics, the first women's Olympic marathon was held.

Who can run a marathon?

Most people with proper training can successfully walk/run 26.2 miles. But before you start a full- or half-marathon training program, remember that it's your health and your body we're talking about. Be sure to speak with your family doctor about your exercise aspirations before starting any vigorous training program. If you have, or have had, an injury that may interfere with your marathon goal, read Chapter 8 on common injuries and recovery, and be sure to discuss any concerns with your doctor or health care provider.

How long will it take me to prepare to run a half or full marathon?

This is a difficult question to answer because not all beginning runners are the same. Body type, fitness level and exposure to sport all impact your ability to run. That said, running experts suggest that if you are able to run a 10-k distance and have consistently run this distance once a week for two weeks, along with two other runs, it is likely that you can handle a half-marathon training program. Most half-marathon programs last approximately 15 weeks.

If your goal is to run a full marathon, it's important to know that most seasoned runners suggest completing a half-marathon training program before attempting the 26.2-mile training regime. In order to be ready to begin one of the many 24- to 30-week marathon training programs, running expert and Canadian Olympian Lynn Kanuka suggests that you need to have been running consistently three times a week for two months and to have been comfortable running about 10 k once a week during the last few weeks of that time before you are ready to embark on the half- or full-marathon journey.

RUNNER PROFILE

Kelly

A few years ago, Kelly made the move from the sidelines to the race. She had always been a big supporter of her husband, Fred, and his athletic achievements. But this year, Kelly and her girlfriend followed the 13-week walk/run program. They enjoyed training so much that they decided to increase the distance of their long weekend run with the intention of completing a half marathon. Kelly then managed to walk/run the half marathon in two hours. She enjoyed crossing the finish line, but more than that she loved the training, especially the feeling of pushing her limits both physically and psychologically.

Kelly had always thought that distance runners were skinny and super fit with type-A personalities. But after completing the half marathon, she realized that distance runners come in all shapes, sizes and personality types, though Kelly isn't sure if she'll attempt a full marathon in the future. For now, she's enjoying her three weekly runs with her dog, Betsy, and her girlfriend, Margie.

What is a reasonable length of time to run a marathon?

There is no such thing as a reasonable time to run a marathon. Male elite runners finish in and around 2 hours, while top female runners cross the finish line in 2 hours and 20 minutes. Still, it is not uncommon for people to walk/run portions of the marathon and complete the distance in 4 to 6 hours.

Is this a healthy and safe endeavor?

Again, this is a difficult question. The information outlined above is a good guide to understanding the level of fitness required to train for longer distances. However, if you are over the age of 30 and have had limited exposure to running and fitness, you need to check with your health care provider to ensure that training for a half or full marathon is a safe and healthy goal.

What does it mean to pace myself?

Pacing is the process of finding a pace that you can maintain throughout your training run. This is not as easy as it sounds; finding the right pace can be difficult. All too often beginning runners take the "no pain, no gain" approach. But in the early stages of training or when participating in events, it's important to go slowly and remember that running too fast can lead to fatigue and, possibly, physical breakdown. Even the most accomplished runners often start out fast in a distance event, only to find they have nothing left in the tank for the last few miles of the race. It should feel relatively easy for the first while and you should be able to maintain a conversation.

Will running this distance be too challenging?

Regardless of whether you're an elite or beginning runner, training for and completing a half or full marathon to the best of your ability and fitness level is difficult and demanding. If you are serious about this commitment, one of the key elements in meeting your challenge is learning to cope with exhausting discomfort. And, you will have to learn to distinguish between the feeling that goes with pushing yourself to perform your best and the pain that is linked to injury. By following a proper half- or full-marathon training program, you will familiarize yourself with the feelings of fatigue and the minor aches associated with a new activity. Of course, as any marathoner will tell you, the feeling that comes with crossing the finish line after 26.2 miles more than makes up for all of the pain and fatigue.

RUNNER PROFILE

Andy

Andy is six-foot-two and 220 pounds (99 kg). Before embarking on his first half marathon, this 40-year-old was concerned that his large frame would be a barrier to achieving his running goal. Andy had always thought of marathoners as people with extremely slight frames. However, using the 13-week walk/run program, he set his sights on running a half marathon. The 13-week schedule is geared toward running a 10-k race, a little less than his 13.1-mile (21-kilometer) goal. So with the help of the guys at the local running store, Andy reworked the 13-week schedule to incorporate a longer run each weekend in order to prepare him for the half-marathon distance. An additional inspiration for Andy was his friend, Seth, who recently had a near-death experience and underwent a liver transplant. He had also just completed a full marathon.

Andy's commitment and perseverance in completing the half-marathon training program paid off. Andy had no problem finishing his half marathon and he did it in a much faster time than he had thought possible. Andy's next running goal is to complete a full marathon with his pal, Seth.

What does it mean to hit the wall?

Hitting the wall is a common phrase used by marathon runners when referring to a point in a race when they run out of energy. Basically, you have hit the wall when your fuel supply no longer meets your energy demands. The runner who hits the wall has two choices: drop out of the race or slow down and endure the discomfort of tight and burning muscles until reaching the finish line.

According to marathon expert and author Jeff Galloway, approximately 40 per cent of all non-elite marathon runners have hit the wall. The good news is that this can easily be avoided with good pre-race nutrition, proper hydration and suitable nutrition throughout the race.

Reasons for running a half or full marathon

Every runner has their own reasons for training for a half or full marathon, but here are a few of the most common:

- You want a new challenge
- You think it's doable
- Others have done it, and you're inspired and challenged by that
- There's a mystique around the marathoner
- You like the idea of making a serious commitment to a running program
- Your friend wants a running partner
- You're in a midlife crisis and need to be a little crazy
- You want to take charge of your life, and running a marathon would mark a turning point for you

Why is core strength important?

- Strong back muscles increase your comfort level when walking or jogging
- Strong back muscles are helped by strong stomach muscles
- A gradual walk/jog program will naturally increase core strength and, therefore, improve your running technique
- If you have a weakness in your back or stomach, a good core strength fitness program is helpful; yoga, pilates and aerobics are great for this

—Olympian Lynn Kanuka

Building Blocks for a Half and Full Marathon

New runners, or anyone who has been running regularly for less than six months, should not feel pressured to train for long distances like a half or full marathon. If you have already completed the 13-week walk/run training program outlined earlier in this book, there are a variety of ways to maintain or improve your running fitness without training for a marathon.

Even the most seasoned runners need to look for ways to stay motivated and on track with their running goals. Ask at your local community center about running groups or find a friend who might be interested in joining you for one of your runs. Choosing an upcoming 5- or 10-k race is another great motivator. And if you still have your heart fixed on a marathon or half marathon, you won't be alone. As track-and-field Olympian Lynn Kanuka says, "I

RUNNER PROFILE

Peter

Peter had let himself get extremely out of shape. The 41-year-old lawyer wanted to lose the extra weight around his midsection and get back to the fitness level he was at 10 years ago.

Peter knew that in order for this to happen he had to really commit himself to a regular fitness schedule. Last spring, he and his wife, Stella, joined a 13-week walk/run clinic and trained for a 10-k race. After the race, his wife thought he was crazy when he told her he was going to run a half marathon in six months. But two months into his running program, his wife realized he was serious and became his biggest supporter. When the weather turned cold, she would encourage him with promises of a hearty breakfast and hot coffee after his long weekend runs.

Peter managed to stick with his schedule and recently completed his first half marathon. He then took the suggested week of rest, but after seven days away from running he was definitely ready to return to his regular morning runs.

have never run a half or full marathon myself, but I definitely recognize that there is a mystique about completing one. I have an inner tug every so often toward the idea of doing one, but for me, as a single working mother and someone who's predisposed to stress fractures, I have to be realistic about the time demands of training for a marathon as well as my physical limitations."

The basis of any half- or full-marathon program is to build a strong foundation of consistent running. Nothing fancy: just back-to-back weeks of progressive training and a slow increase in running time will improve your endurance and gradually develop your mental and physical strength. These are two of the key elements needed to train successfully for the distances involved in both half and full marathons.

Training to Run a Half Marathon

The eight-week training schedule outlined on page 204 for building up to a half or full marathon is for beginning and intermediate runners. You have already trained to complete a 10 k—a feat in itself. The next step is to become comfortable with a weekly long run of 10 k. You need to be comfortable with this long run over the course of several consecutive weeks before you embark on the half-marathon journey.

Based on the principles described in earlier chapters, the eight-week schedule recommends one longer run and two or three shorter runs per week as well as an interval training session for the run-faster folks. The interval session helps build muscle and strength endurance while adding variety to your training. The long runs help to build cardiovascular fitness and familiarize your body with the increased stress that comes with long-distance running.

When you review the 8-week training program, you will notice that we have included suggested running times as well as specific distances. Take a drive and measure the various running routes using your car's odometer. It is important to gradually build your mental and physical strength. By measuring the distance of your training runs, you avoid overtraining (running farther than necessary). The pace for your first-time experience is irrelevant. It's all about respecting and preparing for the distance. Be

Mindy

Six hours, twenty-two minutes and seven seconds. That's how long it took Mindy to run the Vancouver International Marathon in Vancouver, British Columbia.

Mindy had never thought of herself as an athlete. "But I spent the last eight months working my behind off with 100 other women to run a marathon—a feat that we all thought was insurmountable."

Mindy also hadn't seen herself as a runner, and says she has never had the runner's build. "It's hard to believe that I bought my first pair of runners last year. During my adolescence, I was considered chubby or, as my mother would say, "cuddly." I was extremely sedentary and always loved to bake and eat." But when Mindy's brother, Ted, started running in the mornings, she was amazed at how excited he was about his new-found fitness. Mindy decided to walk when her brother went jogging. Then one day he suggested she try to jog with him for the first five minutes. After that, Mindy was hooked.

It took Mindy a month or so before she could jog the 30-minute route with her brother, but she did it. Soon after, she began dreaming about running a marathon. "I love running with my brother, but he didn't have any interest in the marathon so it was great for me to join a group of women who had a shared goal. I don't think I could have done it without their support.

aware that in each session you are running the approximate distance indicated for that workout. Each session will bring you closer to covering the half-marathon distance. On race day, you will then have the knowledge, confidence and peace of mind that you can and will complete the race.

Keep in mind that this training schedule is flexible. It's up to you to decide which days of the week you will do each of your runs. However, it makes sense to space your runs out through each week. As discussed earlier, you may also want to consider meeting a friend who runs at a similar pace for the occasional run. This helps with motivation, but can also make training more fun. You can also ensure that your easy runs are at a talking pace.

Appendix A

Sample Training Log

WEEK 6		Workout	Notes (e.g., weather, temperature, how I felt)
	Sunday	Rest day	
	Monday	Rest day	
	Tuesday	Medium run—41 minutes	Tonight it was clear and crisp. I ran with the dog and felt a bit tired—I must still be recovering from Saturday's long run. I'm glad I have tomorrow off.
	Wednesday	Rest day	
	Thursday	Long run—46 minutes	Ran this morning with Rachel and saw a beautiful sunrise. Felt great. All the leg fatigue I felt on Tuesday's run had disappeared.
	Friday	Rest day	
	Saturday	Long run—50 minutes	Ran with Maddy and Thom before the kids got up. It was sunny but cool. We chatted for most of the run, and I was surprised when we had only 5 minutes to go. I could have run longer. This is amazing because this was the first week I ran 3 semi-long runs. I must be getting fitter!

Appendix B

The 13-Week Walk Program

If you're not interested in running—or if injury prevents you from running—you may wish to consider this walking program. Walking offers an excellent form of cardiovascular exercise that uses large muscle groups and provides weight-bearing activity.

Remember, this is not a stroll! Building up to walking at a brisk pace (about 10 minutes per 3/4 mile/about 1 kilometer) will require some effort. You'll have to reschedule stopping to feed the ducks or chatting with the neighbors for another time.

Note that the times shown do not include your 10-minute warm-up and 10-minute cool-down in each training session. Be sure to allow extra time in your schedule for these essential components of your training.

WEEK 1

Session 1	12 minutes	A 3-minute brisk walk followed by a 2-minute slow and easy recovery walk. A 2-minute brisk walk followed by a 2-minute slow and easy recovery walk. A 1-minute brisk walk followed by a 2-minute slow and easy recovery walk.
Session 2	15 minutes	Walk 15 minutes.
Session 3	20 minutes	Walk 20 minutes.

WEEK 2

Session 1	16 minutes	A 2-minute brisk walk followed by a 2-minute slow and easy recovery walk. Repeat this combination 4 times.
Session 2	20 minutes	Walk 20 minutes.
Session 3	30 minutes	Walk 30 minutes.

WEEK 3

Session 1	24 minutes	A 1-minute brisk walk followed by a 2-minute slow and easy recovery walk. Repeat this combination 8 times.
Session 2	30 minutes	Walk 30 minutes.
Session 3	40 minutes	Walk 40 minutes.

WEEK 4

Session 1	12 minutes	A 3-minute brisk walk followed by a 2-minute slow and easy recovery walk. A 2-minute brisk walk followed by a 2-minute recovery walk. A 1-minute brisk walk followed by a 2-minute recovery walk.
Session 2	20 minutes	Walk 20 minutes.
Session 3	30 minutes	Walk 30 minutes.

WEEK 5

Session 1	21 minutes	A 5-minute brisk walk followed by a 2-minute slow and easy recovery walk. Repeat this combination 3 times.
Session 2	30 minutes	Walk 30 minutes.
Session 3	40 minutes	Walk 40 minutes.

WEEK 6

Session 1	36 minutes	A 3-minute brisk walk followed by a 2-minute slow and easy recovery walk. A 2-minute brisk walk followed by a 2-minute slow and easy recovery walk. A 1-minute brisk walk followed by a 2-minute slow and easy recovery walk. Repeat this three-part combination 3 times.
Session 2	30 minutes	Walk 30 minutes.
Session 3	50 minutes	Walk 50 minutes.

WEEK 7

Session 1	36 minutes	A 3-minute brisk walk followed by a 3-minute slow and easy recovery walk. Repeat this combination 6 times.
Session 2	40 minutes	Walk 40 minutes.
Session 3	60 minutes	Walk 60 minutes.

WEEK 8 (Easy Recovery Week)

Session 1	30 minutes	A 1-minute brisk walk followed by a 2-minute slow and easy recovery walk. Repeat this combination 10 times.
Session 2	30 minutes	Walk 30 minutes.
Session 3	40 minutes	Walk 40 minutes.

WEEK 9

Session 1	32 minutes	A 6-minute brisk walk followed by a 2-minute slow and easy recovery walk. A 3-minute brisk walk followed by a 2-minute recovery walk. A 1-minute brisk walk followed by a 2-minute recovery walk. Repeat this three-part combination 2 times.
Session 2	40 minutes	Walk 40 minutes.
Session 3	60 minutes	Walk 60 minutes.

WEEK 10

Session 1	24 minutes	A 4-minute brisk walk followed by a 2-minute slow and easy recovery walk. Repeat this combination 4 times.
Session 2	50 minutes	Walk 50 minutes.
Session 3	70 minutes	Walk 70 minutes.

WEEK 11

Session 1	30 minutes (approximately)	Find a hill that has an incline of approximately 25 degrees. Walk uphill briskly for 1 minute then walk back down at a slow and easy recovery pace. Repeat this combination 8 times. Next, on the same hill: Walk uphill briskly for 30 seconds then walk back down at a slow and easy recovery pace. Repeat this combination 8 times. *If there is no hill available:* A 90-second brisk walk followed by a 2-minute slow and easy recovery walk. Repeat this combination 6 times. Next: A 45-second brisk walk followed by a 2-minute slow and easy recovery walk. Repeat this combination 6 times.
Session 2	40 minutes	Walk 40 minutes.
Session 3	60 minutes	Walk 60 minutes.

WEEK 12

Session 1	45 minutes	A 5-minute brisk walk followed by a 2-minute slow and easy recovery walk. A 3-minute brisk walk followed by a 2-minute slow and easy recovery walk. A 1-minute brisk walk followed by a 2-minute slow and easy recovery walk. Repeat this three-part combination 3 times.
Session 2	40 minutes	Walk 40 minutes.
Session 3	80 minutes	Walk 80 minutes.

WEEK 13

Session 1	24 minutes	A 3-minute brisk walk followed by a 2-minute slow and easy recovery walk. A 2-minute brisk walk followed by a 2-minute slow and easy recovery walk. A 1-minute brisk walk followed by a 2-minute slow and easy recovery walk. Repeat this three-part combination 2 times.
Session 2	40 minutes	Walk 40 minutes.
Session 3		Race Day: See you at the finish line!

Appendix C

The 13-Week Run Faster Program

This program is designed for people who have completed the 13-week walk/run program and would like to increase their running endurance and intensity in a safe and effective way. Anyone following this program should be sure to allow at least one rest (or cross-training) day between any two running sessions.

Note that the times shown do not include your 10-minute warm-up and 10-minute cool-down in each training session. Be sure to allow extra time in your schedule for these essential components of your training.

WEEK 1

Session 1	12 minutes	A 3-minute brisk run* followed by a 2-minute slow and easy recovery jog.
		A 2-minute brisk run followed by a 2-minute slow and easy recovery jog.
		A 1-minute brisk run followed by a 2-minute slow and easy recovery jog.
Session 2	20 minutes	Run 20 minutes.
Session 3	25 minutes	Run 25 minutes.

*Brisk running means you cannot speak any more than two sentences at one time; if you can say more than two sentences you're going too slow; any less and you're going too fast.

WEEK 2

Session 1	16 minutes	A 2-minute brisk run followed by a 2-minute slow and easy recovery jog. Repeat this combination 4 times.
Session 2	20 minutes	Run 20 minutes.
Session 3	25 minutes	Run 25 minutes.

WEEK 3

Session 1	24 minutes	A 1-minute brisk run followed by a 2-minute slow and easy recovery jog. Repeat this combination 8 times.
Session 2	25 minutes	Run 25 minutes.
Session 3	25 minutes	Run 25 minutes.

WEEK 4 (Easy Recovery Week)

Session 1	12 minutes	A 3-minute brisk run followed by a 2-minute slow and easy recovery jog.
		A 2-minute brisk run followed by a 2-minute slow and easy recovery jog.
		A 1-minute brisk run followed by a 2-minute slow and easy recovery jog.
Session 2	20 minutes	Run 20 minutes.
Session 3	20 minutes	Run 20 minutes.

WEEK 5

Session 1	14 minutes	A 5-minute brisk run followed by a 2-minute slow and easy recovery jog.
		Repeat this combination 2 times.
Session 2	20 minutes	Run 20 minutes.
Session 3	30 minutes	Run 30 minutes.

WEEK 6

Session 1	24 minutes	A 3-minute brisk run followed by a 2-minute slow and easy recovery jog.
		A 2-minute brisk run followed by a 2-minute slow and easy recovery jog.
		A 1-minute brisk run followed by a 2-minute slow and easy recovery jog.
		Repeat this three-part combination 2 times.
Session 2	20 minutes	Run 20 minutes.
Session 3	35 minutes	Run 35 minutes.

WEEK 7

Session 1	30 minutes	A 3-minute brisk run followed by a 3-minute slow and easy recovery jog.
		Repeat this combination 5 times.
Session 2	20 minutes	Run 20 minutes.
Session 3	40 minutes	Run 40 minutes.

WEEK 8 (Easy Recovery Week)

Session 1	27.5 minutes	A 1-minute brisk run followed by a 2-minute slow and easy recovery jog.
		A 30-second brisk run followed by a 2-minute slow and easy recovery jog.
		Repeat this two-part combination 5 times.
Session 2	20 minutes	Run 20 minutes.
Session 3	20 minutes	Run 20 minutes.

WEEK 9

Session 1	25 minutes	A 5-minute brisk run followed by a 2-minute slow and easy recovery jog.
		A 4-minute brisk run followed by a 2-minute slow and easy recovery jog.
		A 3-minute brisk run followed by a 2-minute slow and easy recovery jog.
		A 2-minute brisk run followed by a 2-minute slow and easy recovery jog.
		A 1-minute brisk run followed by a 2-minute slow and easy recovery jog.
Session 2	20 minutes	Run 20 minutes.
Session 3	45 minutes	Run 45 minutes.

WEEK 10

Session 1	24 minutes	A 2-minute brisk run followed by a 2-minute slow and easy recovery jog. Repeat this combination 6 times.
Session 2	20 minutes	Run 20 minutes.
Session 3	50 minutes	Run 50 minutes.

WEEK 11

Session 1	25 minutes (approximately)	Find a hill that has an incline of approximately 25 degrees. Run briskly uphill for 1 minute then jog slow and easy back down. Repeat this combination 6 times. Next, on the same hill: Run briskly uphill for 30 seconds then jog slow and easy back down. Repeat this combination 6 times.
		If there is no hill available:
		A 90-second brisk run followed by a 2-minute slow and easy recovery jog. Repeat this combination 6 times.
		A 45-second brisk run followed by a 2-minute slow and easy recovery jog. Repeat this combination 6 times.
Session 2	20 minutes	Run 20 minutes.
Session 3	40 minutes	Run 40 minutes.

WEEK 12

Session 1	30 minutes	A 5-minute brisk run followed by a 2-minute slow and easy recovery jog.
		A 3-minute brisk run followed by a 2-minute slow and easy recovery jog.
		A 1-minute brisk run followed by a 2-minute slow and easy recovery jog.
		Repeat this three-part combination 2 times.
Session 2	20 minutes	Run 20 minutes.
Session 3	50 minutes	Run 50 minutes.

WEEK 13

Session 1	12 minutes	A 3-minute brisk run followed by a 2-minute slow and easy recovery jog.
		A 2-minute brisk run followed by a 2-minute slow and easy recovery jog.
		A 1-minute brisk run followed by a 2-minute slow and easy recovery jog.
Session 2	20 minutes	Run 20 minutes.
Session 3		Race Day: See you at the finish line!

Appendix D

The 13-Week Walk/Run Maintenance Program

This program is designed for people who have completed the 13-week walk/run program and want to maintain their fitness gains by staying active. You may choose to follow this program, a modified version of this program or another program altogether. Whichever you choose, remember that if you have a specific training program to follow you will be more likely to maintain your activity level.

As with the other programs in this book, you will have three training sessions each week. It's best to schedule these throughout the week so that you have at least one day between sessions. Most training sessions will take about an hour to complete.

Note that the times shown do not include your 5-minute warm-up and 5-minute cool-down in each training session. Be sure to allow extra time in your schedule for these essential components of your training.

WEEK 1		
Session 1	42 minutes	Run 4 minutes. Walk 2 minutes. Do this 7 times.
Session 2	48 minutes	Run 4 minutes. Walk 2 minutes. Do this 8 times.
Session 3	48 minutes	Run 4 minutes. Walk 2 minutes. Do this 8 times.

WEEK 2		
Session 1	42 minutes	Walk 5 minutes. Walk 1 minute. Do this 7 times.
Session 2	48 minutes	Run 5 minutes. Walk 1 minute. Do this 8 times.
Session 3	54 minutes	Run 5 minutes. Walk 1 minute. Do this 9 times.

WEEK 3		
Session 1	45 minutes	Run 7 minutes. Walk 2 minutes. Do this 5 times.
Session 2	45 minutes	Run 7 minutes. Walk 2 minutes. Do this 5 times.
Session 3	54 minutes	Run 7 minutes. Walk 2 minutes. Do this 6 times.

WEEK 4

Session 1	44 minutes	Run 10 minutes. Walk 1 minute. Do this 4 times.
Session 2	52 minutes	Run 12 minutes. Walk 1 minute. Do this 4 times.
Session 3	44 minutes	Run 10 minutes. Walk 1 minute. Do this 4 times.

WEEK 5

Session 1	48 minutes	Run 15 minutes. Walk 1 minute. Do this 3 times.
Session 2	51 minutes	Run 16 minutes. Walk 1 minute. Do this 3 times.
Session 3	54 minutes	Run 17 minutes. Walk 1 minute. Do this 3 times.

WEEK 6

Session 1	41 minutes	Run 20 minutes. Walk 1 minute. Run 20 minutes.
Session 2	43 minutes	Run 22 minutes. Walk 1 minute. Run 20 minutes.
Session 3	43 minutes	Run 22 minutes. Walk 1 minute. Run 20 minutes.

WEEK 7

Session 1	30 minutes	Run 30 minutes.
Session 2	30 minutes	Run 30 minutes.
Session 3	35 minutes	Run 35 minutes.

WEEK 8

Session 1	33 minutes	Run 33 minutes.
Session 2	30 minutes	Run 30 minutes.
Session 3	35 minutes	Run 35 minutes.

WEEK 9

Session 1	41 minutes	Run 30 minutes. Walk 1 minute. Run 10 minutes.
Session 2	46 minutes	Run 30 minutes. Walk 1 minute. Run 15 minutes.
Session 3	46 minutes	Run 30 minutes. Walk 1 minute. Run 15 minutes.

WEEK 10

Session 1	46 minutes	Run 35 minutes. Walk 1 minute. Run 10 minutes.
Session 2	51 minutes	Run 30 minutes. Walk 1 minute. Run 20 minutes.
Session 3	51 minutes	Run 30 minutes. Walk 1 minute. Run 20 minutes.

WEEK 11

Session 1	40 minutes	Run 40 minutes.
Session 2	45 minutes	Run 45 minutes.
Session 3	40 minutes	Run 40 minutes.

WEEK 12

Session 1	56 minutes	Run 45 minutes. Walk 1 minute. Run 10 minutes.
Session 2	61 minutes	Run 45 minutes. Walk 1 minute. Run 15 minutes.
Session 3	40 minutes	Run 24 minutes. Walk 1 minute. Run 15 minutes.

WEEK 13

Session 1	35 minutes	Run 35 minutes.
Session 2	40 minutes	Run 40 minutes.
Session 3	60 minutes	Complete a 10-k event (if this is your goal) or run 60 minutes.

Appendix E

The 8-Week Run Farther Program

The 8-week run farther program was designed by Olympian Lynn Kanuka and distance running coach Jerry Tighe. The goal of this program is to prepare beginner and intermediate runners for the demands of training for a half marathon. Before considering this program, it's important to have already completed the 13-week walk/run program and/or be comfortable jogging 10 k.

Note that the times shown do not include your 5-minute warm-up and 5-minute cool-down in each training session. Be sure to allow extra time in your schedule for these important components of your training.

WEEK 1

	RUN	DISTANCE
Session 1	Run 30 minutes continuously.	2.5 miles/4 kilometers
Session 2	Run 20 minutes continuously.	2 miles/3.2 kilometers
Session 3	Run 40 minutes continuously.	3 miles/4.8 kilometers

Note: This should be a nice, comfortable week. The distances are manageable and you should feel excited to get on with the next week—like, "Bring it on, I'm ready for this!"

WEEK 2

	RUN	DISTANCE
Session 1	Run 35 minutes continuously.	3 miles/4.8 kilometers
Session 2	Run 25 minutes continuously.	2 miles/3.2 kilometers
Session 3	Run 45 minutes continuously.	3.75 miles/6 kilometers

Note: Subtle increases in both time spent running; for the run-faster group, an increase in speed. You should not be feeling overtaxed but energized and enthusiastic about this week's accomplishments.

WEEK 3

	RUN	DISTANCE
Session 1	Run 40 minutes continuously.	3.5 miles/6 kilometers
Session 2	Run 25 minutes continuously.	2 miles/3.2 kilometers
Session 3	Run 50 minutes continuously.	4 miles/6.4 kilometers

Note: After three great back-to-back weeks and this week's long run, your confidence is building significantly.

WEEK 4

	RUN	DISTANCE
Session 1	Run 50 minutes continuously.	4 miles/6.4 kilometers
Session 2	Run 35 minutes continuously.	3 miles/4.8 kilometers
Session 3	Run 65 minutes continuously.	5 miles/8 kilometers-plus

Note: In order for you to continue to improve, the program includes a recovery week. Enjoy!

WEEK 5

	RUN	DISTANCE
Session 1	Run 45 minutes continuously.	4 miles/6.4 kilometers
Session 2	Run 35 minutes continuously.	3 miles/4.8 kilometers
Session 3	Run 50 minutes continuously.	4.5 miles/7.2 kilometers

Note: Back to work again. This is your first introduction to a four-session training week. Don't be surprised if the legs are feeling a little tired. Get some extra rest and enjoy a soak in the tub.

WEEK 6

	RUN	DISTANCE
Session 1	Run 35 minutes continuously.	3 miles/4.8 kilometers
Session 2	Run 50 minutes continuously.	4 miles/6.4 kilometers
Session 3	Run 35 minutes continuously.	3 miles/4.8 kilometers
Session 4	Run 60 minutes continuously.	5 miles/8 kilometers

Note: This is an important week with four training sessions, including a good long run. Hopefully your body and mind are becoming accustomed to the workload.

WEEK 7

	RUN	DISTANCE
Session 1	Run 35 minutes continuously.	3 miles/4.8 kilometers
Session 2	Run 50 minutes continuously.	4 miles/6.4 kilometers
Session 3	Run 35 minutes continuously.	3 miles/4.8 kilometers
Session 4	Run 70 minutes continuously.	6 miles/10 kilometers

Note: You should be feeling great, if a little tired. You've come a long way and the idea of training for a half marathon seems less daunting.

WEEK 8

	RUN	DISTANCE
Session 1	Run 35 minutes continuously.	3 miles/4.8 kilometers
Session 2	Run 50 minutes continuously.	4 miles/6.4 kilometers
Session 3	Run 75 minutes continuously.	6 miles-plus/10 kilometers

Note: Congratulations! You now have the tools to handle a half-marathon training program with gusto. Good luck!

For Further Reading

Cross-Training
Books
Moran, Gary T., and George H. McGlynn. *Cross-Training for Sports.* Champaign, Ill.: Human Kinetics, 1997.

Yacenda, John. *Fitness Cross-Training.* Champaign, Ill.: Human Kinetics, 1994.

Articles in popular magazines
Morris, Alfred. "How to Build Cross-Training Programs." *Running & FitNews,* September 1994, 4–5.

Health, Exercise and Physiology
Books
Bouchard, Claude, ed. *Physical Activity, Fitness and Health: International Proceedings and Consensus Statement.* Champaign, Ill.: Human Kinetics, 1994.

Franks, B. *Fitness Facts: The Healthy Living Handbook.* Champaign, Ill.: Human Kinetics, 1989.

Sharkey, Brian J. *Fitness and Health.* 4th ed. Champaign, Ill.: Human Kinetics, 1997.

Articles in journals
Chave, S. P. W., J. N. Morris, S. Moss, and A. M. Semmence. "Vigorous Exercise in Leisure Time and the Death Rate: A Study of Male Civil Servants." *Journal of Epidemiology and Community Health* 32 (1978): 239–43.

Paffenbarger, R. S., R. T. Hyde, D. L. Jung, and A. L. Wing. "Epidemiology of Exercise and Coronary Heart Disease." *Clinics in Sports Medicine* 3, no. 2 (1984): 297–318.

Injury Prevention and Care
Books
Micheli, Lyle J. *Healthy Runner's Handbook.* Champaign, Ill.: Human Kinetics, 1996.

Noakes, T., and S. Granger. *Running Injuries: How to Prevent Them & Overcome Them.* Oxford University Press, 2003.

Articles in journals/books
Macintyre, J. and D. R. Lloyd-Smith. "Intrinsic Factors in Overuse Running Injuries." In *Sports Injuries: Basic Principles of Prevention and Care,* edited by P. Renstrom, 139–60. International Olympic Committee Encyclopedia Series no. 4. Oxford: Blackwell Scientific Publications, 1993.

Articles in popular magazines
"Stretching Reduces Injuries?" *Running & FitNews,* September 1995, 3.

Web sites
Dr. Pribut's Running Injuries Page www.drpribut.com/sports/sportframe.html

The Physician and Sportsmedicine www.physsportsmed.com

Runner's World www.runnersworld.com/

Marathons and Half Marathons
Books
Bingham, John. *Marathoning for Mortals.* Rodale Books, 2003.

Motivation and Psychology
Books
Farres, L. and Sport Medicine Council of B.C. *The Beginning Runner's Journal.* Greystone Books, 2003.

Orlick, Terry. *In Pursuit of Excellence: How to Win in Life and Sport Through Mental Training.* Champaign, Ill.: Human Kinetics, 2000.

Sheehan, George A. *Running and Being: The Total Experience.* New York: Simon and Schuster, 1978.

Articles in popular magazines
Beverly, Jonathan. "Breaking Free." *Runner's World,* November 1997, 70–72.

Nutrition
Books
Chuey, Patricia. *The 101 Most Asked Nutrition Questions.* Vancouver: Eating for Energy, 1999.

Clark, Nancy. *Nancy Clark's Sports Nutrition Guidebook.* Champaign, Ill.: Human Kinetics, 2003.

Coleman, Ellen. *Eating for Endurance.* Bull Publishing, 2003.

Havala, S. and M. Clifford. *Simple, Low Fat and Vegetarian.* Gordon Soules Book Publishers, 1999.

Hawley, John, and L. Burke. *Peak Performance: Training & Nutritional Strategies for Sport.* Independant Publishers Groups, 1998.

Journals
University of California at Berkeley Wellness Letter: The Newsletter of Nutrition, Fitness and Stress Management. Health Letter Associates, P.O. Box 420235, Palm Coast, Florida, 32142. Toll Free 1-800-829-9080.

Articles in popular magazines
"R$_x$—Fruits, Veggies and Dairy Products." *Running & FitNews,* July 1998, 1.

Web sites
American Dietetic Association www.eatright.org

Gatorade Sports Science Institute www.gssiweb.com

Health Canada Nutrition Online Service www.hc-sc.gc.ca/hppb/nutrition

National Council Against Health Fraud www.ncahf.org

Runner's World www.runnersworld.com

United States Department of Agriculture, Food and Nutrition Information Center www.nal.usda.gov/fnic

The Vegetarian Resource Group www.vrg.org

Race Preparation and Beyond
Books
Glover, Bob, and Jack Shepherd. *The Runner's Handbook: The Best-Selling Classic Fitness Guide for Beginner and Intermediate Runners.* New York: Penguin Books, 1996.

Henderson, Joe, and Jeff Galloway. *Better Runs: 25 Years' Worth of Lessons for*

Running Faster and Farther. Champaign, Ill.: Human Kinetics, 1995.

Shorter, Frank, with Mike Bloom. *Olympic Gold: A Runner's Life and Times*. Boston: Houghton Mifflin, 1984.

Articles in popular magazines

Douglas, Scott. "Sticking with It for the Long Haul." *Running & FitNews*, December 1992, 4–5.

Galloway, Jeff. "Worry-Free Racing." *Runner's World*, June 1998, 42.

Web sites

RunCoach Running Tips www.sportscoach.com.au/ tipindex.html

Running (General)
Books

Bigham, John. *The Courage to Start: A Guide to Running for Your Life*. New York: Simon & Shuster, 1999.

Burfoot, Amby, ed. *Runner's World Complete Book of Running: Everything You Need to Know to Run for Fun, Fitness and Competition*. Emmaus, Pa.: Rodale Books, 2004.

Fixx, James F. *The Complete Book of Running*. New York: Random House, 1977.

Galloway, Jeff. *Galloway's Book on Running*. Bolinas, Cal.: Shelter Publications, 2002.

Glover, Bob et al. *The Runner's Handbook: The Best-Selling Classic Fitness Guide for Beginner and Intermediate Runners*. New York: Penguin Books, 1996.

Kowalchuk, Claire. *The Complete Book of Running for Women*. Mountainview, CA: Two A's Publishing, 1999.

Micheli, Lyle. *Healthy Runner's Handbook*. Champaign, Ill.: Human Kinetics, 1996.

Noakes, Timothy. *Lore of Running*. 4th ed. Champaign, Ill.: Human Kinetics, 2002.

Pftisinger, Pete, and Douglas Scott. *Advanced Marathoning*.

Switzer, Kathryn. *Running and Walking for Women Over 40*. New York: Griffin, 1998.

Popular magazines

Runner's World
Women's Running

Web sites

Runner's World www.runnersworld.com
Runner's World for Women www.womens-running.com
Kick!Links www.kicksports.com

Strength Training
Books

Fleck, Steven J., and William J. Kraemer. *Designing Resistance Training Programs*. 2d ed. Champaign, Ill.: Human Kinetics, 1997.

Peterson, James A., Cedric X. Bryant, and Susan L. Peterson. *Strength Training for Women*. Champaign, Ill.: Human Kinetics, 1995.

Baechle, Thomas R., and Barney R. Groves. *Weight Training: Steps to Success*. 2d ed. Champaign, Ill.: Human Kinetics, 1998.

Stretching and Flexibility

Books

Alter, Michael J. *Science of Flexibility*. 2d ed. Champaign, Ill.: Human Kinetics, 1996.

Alter, Michael J. *Sport Stretch*. 2d ed. Champaign, Ill.: Human Kinetics, 1997.

Stark, Steven. *The Stark Reality of Stretching*. Vancouver: Stark Reality Corp., 1999.

Other Books

Nordahl, K. *Fit to Deliver*. International, 2000.

Index

runner's knee, 136–37
running shoes, 23, 24–26, 72–73,
    126, 178
running technique, 39–40, 94–96,
    126–27, 187

safety, 40–42, 44; *see also* children and
    exercise; medical conditions and
    exercise; pregnancy and exercise
self-worth, 12, 15, 29, 48, 53–54, 57
Sheehan, George, 136
shin pain, 141–42
shin splints. *See* tibial stress syndrome
Smith, Trent, 75
snacking, 117–18
soreness in muscles, 9, 38, 91, 143
Spitz, Mark, 82
sport beverages, 102, 122
sport energy bars, 102, 118
sport medicine practitioners, 126, 131
sports bras, 27–28, 65, 66, 72, 73
strength training, 89–93
strength training exercises, 158–60
stress fractures, 19, 142–43
stress management, 11, 14, 15,
    51–52, 125
stretching, 33, 35–39, 93
stretching exercises, 156–57
supination, 24
surfaces for running, 22, 25, 126, 178
swelling of injuries, 132, 133, 134, 135
swimming, 65, 84–85

Taunton, Jack, 149
technique. *See* running technique
tempo running, 168, 173–74
tendinitis. *See* Achilles tendinitis
tension and running, 39, 96
13-week run faster program, 161–62,
    197–200
13-week walk program, 193–96
13-week walk/run maintenance pro-
    gram, 201–3

13-week walk/run program, 1, 2, 31–32,
    152–55
tibial stress syndrome, 141–42
Tighe, Jerry, 204
time for exercise, 29, 47, 53, 58, 59, 167
training log, 32–34, 52, 127, 151, 192
triathlons, 81, 122, 177

ultra marathons, 81, 183

varicose veins, 13
vegetarian/vegan diets, 99, 102, 111
visualization, 56–57, 147, 178
vitamins, 103, 109–11, 112, 115

walking, 3, 26, 94, 95
walking program, 193–96
warming up, 34–36, 54–55
water, 119–22, 123; *see also* fluid balance
weather and running, 26–27, 28, 32, 43,
    58, 120, 122, 130, 131, 172, 179
weight control, 11–12, 82–83, 85, 103,
    108, 109, 116–17, 119, 123–24; *see also*
    low-carbohydrate diets
weight training. *See* strength training

yoga, 65